THE GREAT ATLAS OF DISCOVERY

Illustrated by Peter Morter
Written by Neil Grant

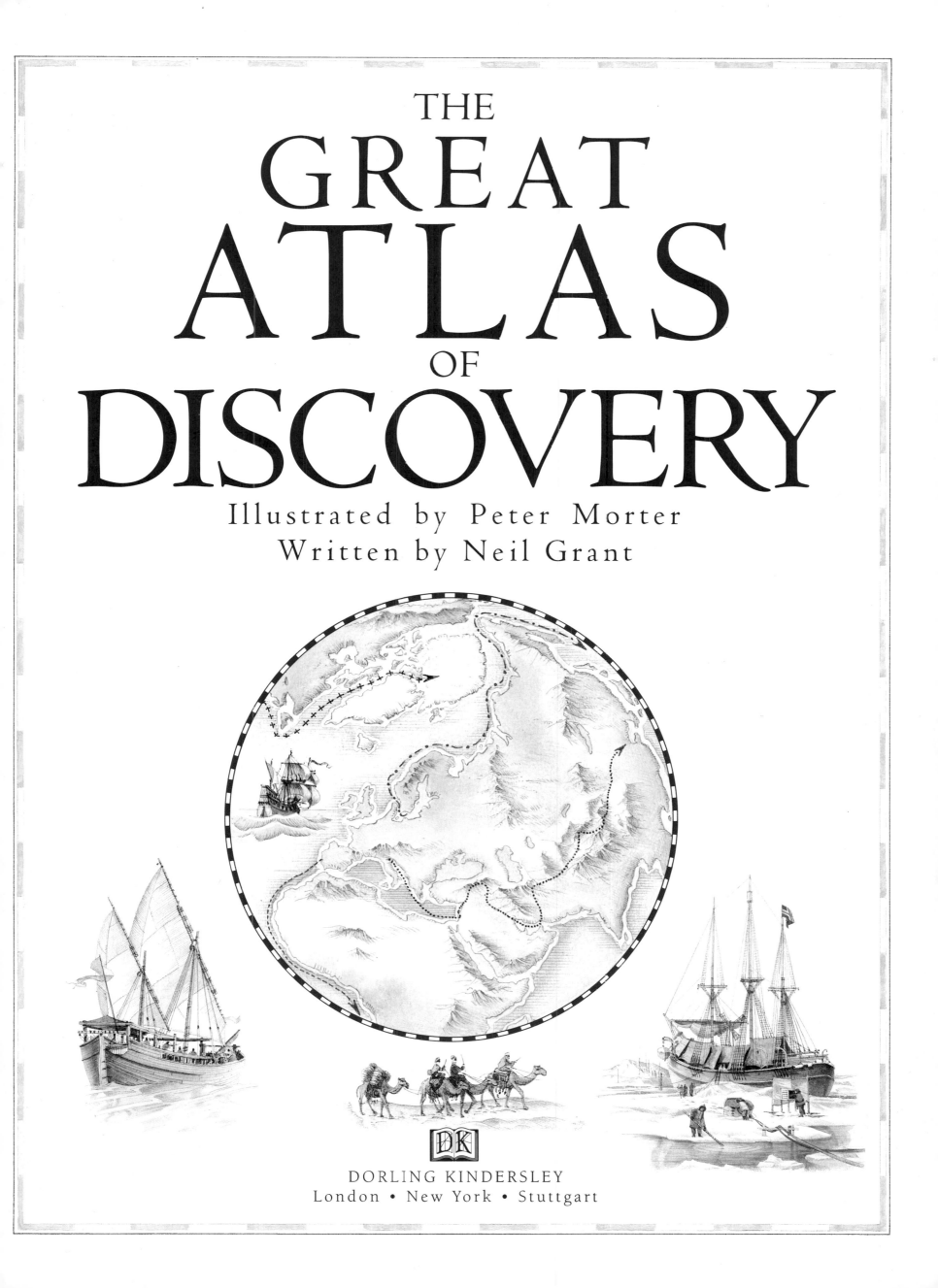

DK

DORLING KINDERSLEY
London • New York • Stuttgart

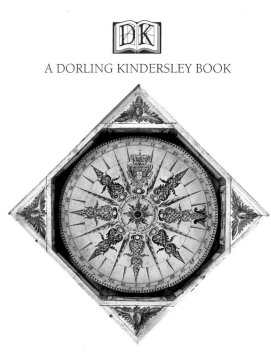

DK

A DORLING KINDERSLEY BOOK

Art Editor Rachael Foster
Project Editor Anderley Moore

Managing Art Editor Jacquie Gulliver
Managing Editor Ann Kramer

Production Marguerite Fenn

First published in Great Britain in 1992
by Dorling Kindersley Limited
9 Henrietta Street, London WC2E 8PS

A CIP catalogue record is available
from the British Library

ISBN   0-86318-830-3

Reproduced by GRB, Verona, Italy
Printed and bound by New Interlitho, Milan, Italy

CONTENTS

HOW TO FOLLOW THE MAPS

THE ATLAS TELLS THE story of exploration, from earliest travellers of the ancient world through to modern space voyagers. It is organised in date order (as far as possible). Most of the double pages feature a detailed map which shows the routes taken by various explorers and the places they visited. The routes are numbered so that you can trace the explorers' footsteps, learning about their adventures along the way. The map and the information around it combine to give full details of important discoveries and the explorers who made them. Although the atlas is mostly made up of maps, it also features subjects such as navigation, trade, and exploring the oceans.

Where on Earth?
On each map there is a globe. The shaded area of the globe shows the location in the world of the country or continent featured.

Compass
Each map has a compass on it so you can see in which direction the explorers are travelling.

Portrait dates
When exact dates are unknown, c. (circa) indicates that the date given is approximate.

Mapping the unknown
Old maps show what people thought lands looked like before explorers returned from their travels with more information to make accurate maps.

Scale
Using the scale as a guide, you can measure the distances explorers travelled on their expeditions.

Key box
This provides the key to the map. Each explorer's route has been given a different colour, pattern and symbol so that you can follow it across the map from start to finish. Dates are included for each expedition.

Symbols
Each explorer has a different style of symbol (e.g circle, square, diamond etc). The symbols are numbered in sequence along the route so that you can read the captions in order.

Where an expedition begins, the number is shown in a solid black symbol e.g ▇

When explorers make more than one expedition, or where two explorers travelling together, split up, the start of the "new" expedition is also shown in a solid black symbol e.g ▇

GUIDE TO THE MAPS

Towns and cities are marked with a dot. Only towns or cities that feature in the explorers' expeditions are shown on the maps.

When the name of a place has changed from that referred to in explorers' journals, the modern name is given first and the old name is in brackets.

Places in inverted commas are those that no longer exist. For example, Christopher Columbus's settlement of "Navidad", which is not there any more.

Rivers that are relevant to the explorers are marked. Where the old name differs from the modern, it is given in brackets.

When the exact location of a place is unknown, a question mark follows the place name. This shows that it is likely, but not certain, that this is where the place was.

The adventures of the explorers are brought to life through beautifully painted scenes.

THE URGE TO EXPLORE

SINCE THE EARLIEST TIMES, people have explored their surroundings. They have crossed the hottest deserts, climbed the highest mountains, and sailed the widest seas. They have struggled through steamy jungle to find an unknown plant and brought back weird creatures from the ocean floor. Today, a new adventure in exploration is beginning. We are finding out about the surroundings of the Earth itself. Already men have walked on the Moon. Spacecraft travelling through the solar system have sent back news of other planets and one day men and women will follow them.

All explorers have in common the human trait of curiosity. However, curiosity was not the only reason for many journeys of discovery. Explorers always had more practical reasons for setting out, for example to search for land or treasure. Others hoped to find valuable trade or new routes to countries that produced the goods they wanted. Some were missionaries, who felt a duty to convert people to their own religion. Some were fishermen or miners or merchants, looking for a better living.

Myths and mistakes
Before people began to understand more about different parts of the world they believed in some very strange stories. They found it hard to tell fact from fiction. If such an amazing beast as an elephant existed, why not an eagle so large it could pick up an elephant in its talons? Early explorers were especially brave because they had to face so many frightening superstitions and legends. Five hundred years ago sailors feared that if they sailed too far across the ocean, their ship might disappear over the edge of the Earth and fall into hell. The Portuguese who started to explore the coast of Africa in the 15th century feared that when they reached the equator the Sun might turn them black and make the sea boil.

Claiming new lands
When Europeans began to explore the world in the 15th century, they often acted as if it belonged to them. When they reached a land where the people seemed primitive to them because they were not Christians, they took over the land on behalf of their own king and country. The result of this, centuries later, was that a large part of the world, including all of North and South America and most of Africa, became European colonies. In most cases, this had terrible consequences for local people.

Trade
There is a saying that "trade follows the flag". In other words when explorers find new lands, traders will soon follow. However, it would be better to say that "the flag follows trade"! It was the search for trade and trade routes that resulted in Europe's discovery of all the world's oceans and continents during the 15th and 16th centuries. The famous voyages of explorers, such as Columbus and Magellan, arose from the desire of Europeans to find a sea route to the markets of the Far East, where valuable goods like silk and spices could be bought. Columbus did not set out to discover a new continent. He was hoping to reach China and Japan, and died insisting that he had done so. Magellan did not intend to sail around the world. He was hoping to find a new route for trade with the Moluccas, or Spice Islands.

Map-making
Most European maps in the Middle Ages show the world as a flat disc. Only three continents are shown – Europe, Asia and Africa, as the existence of the Americas was unknown. The top of the map is East, and at the exact centre of the world is Jerusalem, the Holy City. Jerusalem is placed at the centre of the Earth because that is where the Bible says it is. Maps such as these were usually published in religious books, and we should really think of them not as maps, but as religious pictures. The Christian Church taught that the Earth is flat. Although the Ancient Greeks knew better, and this knowledge never quite died out, most people believed without question that the Earth was flat.

Religion
Unlike many other religions, Christianity claims to be universal. Sincere Christians therefore believed it was their duty to convert other people to Christianity. European expeditions to the Americas included priests, whose job was not only to hold services for the European members of the expedition, but also to convert the local people. Priests of the Jesuit order (founded in 1540) were especially active as missionaries, both in the Americas and in the Far East. One of them, St Francis Xavier, was the first European to visit Japan and another, Father Marquette, discovered the Mississippi River.

ANCIENT EXPLORERS

FROM THE EARLIEST TIMES, human beings have been travellers. Prehistoric peoples travelled in search of better hunting grounds, or to escape the glaciers creeping down from the Arctic during the last Ice Age. But the real story of exploration and discovery began with civilization, as people began to settle colonies, build ships, live in cities, and record their findings in books. With the growth of civilization came the need for trade, and although this was the main reason for setting sail to explore new lands, conquest of these lands provided another purpose for expeditions.

The Ancient Egyptians made voyages down the Red Sea nearly 6000 years ago, and the Phoenicians made even longer voyages, as far as Britain and Africa, becoming the greatest explorers of their age. Later, the Romans also pushed the boundaries of their empire into unknown territory.

The Phoenicians
Phoenicia was a group of city states, occupying a small region of the Syrian coastal plain. By about 1000 BC the Phoenicians had become the greatest sailors of the Mediterranean. Their ships, which were powered by oars and a single sail, were short, broad and strong. They were built from the best timber in the Mediterranean – cedar from the slopes of the Lebanon Mountains, which was also a valuable Phoenician export.

The Pharaoh hires a Phoenician crew
There is a story told by an Ancient Greek historian, Herodotus, about the Egyptian Pharaoh, Necho II. It tells how, in 600 BC, Necho hired a Phoenician crew to make a voyage of exploration from the Red Sea, around Africa and back to Egypt via the Mediterranean – a distance of 25,000 km. The voyage is said to have taken three years because the Phoenicians stopped every year to sow grain and reap the harvest. Many historians doubt this story, but how did Herodotus know it was possible to sail around Africa if no one had done it?

THULE?

ICELAND

NORWAY

Pytheas sails to "Thule", an island about 6 days' sail from the Orkneys.

ORKNEY ISLANDS

THULE?

③

NORTH SEA

SCOTLAND

BRITISH ISLES

IRISH SEA

Pytheas sails across the Irish Sea. He calculates that the north of Scotland is 1,680 km from Massalia. (It is really 1,800 km.) He sees tin miners on the Cornish coast.

④

CORNWALL

Pytheas follows the European coast until he reaches the British Isles. He decides to sail around them.

②

EUROPE

Pytheas leaves Massalia with 2 or 3 ships, c.330 BC. He knows the latitude of Massalia, having measured it by the angle of the moon's shadow.

① MARSEILLES (Massalia)

RC

BALEARIC ISLANDS

MEDITER

CARTHAGE

Hanno leads a fleet of 60 ships from Carthage to look for places on the west coast of Africa where they might start colonies.

SABRATA

The Carthaginians traded with many places in Africa, exchanging textiles a other goods for gold.

ATLANTIC OCEAN

②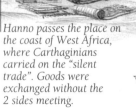

Hanno passes the place on the coast of West Africa, where Carthaginians carried on the "silent trade". Goods were exchanged without the 2 sides meeting.

N

W E

S

AFR

SAF

Hanno sails a short way up the River Senegal where he sees animals that are strange to him.

③ *Senegal*

KEY TO MAP		
VOYAGE TO PUNT	1493 BC	① ⚬⚬⚬⚬⚬
PHOENICIANS	c.600 BC	··········
HANNO	450 BC	▣ + + + +
PYTHEAS	325 BC	① – – – –

Hanno sets out for Africa

The greatest Phoenician voyage that we know about is the voyage of Hanno, in about 500 BC. He led a fleet from Carthage down the west coast of Africa, sailing up the River Senegal and perhaps landing in the Gulf of Guinea. Hanno told of many strange experiences, including a meeting with some "people" who were covered with hair. They were probably chimpanzees.

Traders and colonists

The Phoenician cities of Tyre and Sidon were conquered in about 700 BC, but by that time the Phoenicians had founded many colonies around the Mediterranean. The greatest was Carthage, which became more powerful than either Tyre or Sidon. The Phoenicians traded in many things. They provided timber for Egyptian ships and for King Solomon's temple in Jerusalem. They sailed as far as Cornwall in England to buy tin from the Cornish mines. They also discovered the precious purple dye (called Tyrian purple), which came from a type of shellfish called a murex. The Phoenicians were skilled in metal working and glass blowing, and they developed one of the earliest alphabets.

PYTHEAS

The Greek astronomer, Pytheas, was born in Marseilles, which was then a Greek colony. He made a famous voyage – perhaps two voyages – into the north Atlantic in about 330 BC, probably hoping to break into the Phoenician tin trade. He sailed all round the British Isles and was the first to give an account of the people there, saying that they were friendly. From Scotland he sailed north to a land he called Thule, where, he said, the sun never set. No one knows exactly where Thule was, but this suggests it was close to the Arctic.

Pytheas

The Phoenicians load their ships with wine.

The Phoenicians make Tyre and Sidon their main trading centres.

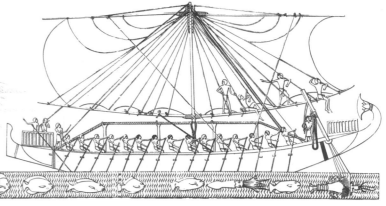

The voyage to Punt

The Ancient Egyptians preferred to live close to the River Nile, but they had to travel in order to trade. About 3,500 years ago, in the reign of Queen Hatshepsut, the Egyptians made a voyage to the Land of Punt (which may have been east Africa). They carried the materials they needed for building ships across the desert from the Nile to the Red Sea – a distance of about 250 km. The voyage, through waters filled with jagged reefs and sharks, took a year or more. Although such voyages had been made at least 500 years earlier, this one was described in words and pictures on the walls of Queen Hatshepsut's temple at Deir el Bahri, near Thebes.

The Egyptian expedition to Punt starts north of Thebes. Everything has to be dragged across the desert to the Red Sea, where their ships are launched.

Riches from Punt

From their expedition to Punt, the Egyptians brought back myrrh and other plants, ivory, ebony, gold, leopard skins, and live animals, such as baboons and pet dogs. The carving (right), in Queen Hatshepsut's temple, shows the Egyptians returning with herbs and spices. The inscription reads "Never was the like brought back to any monarch since the world began".

When Egypt becomes a Roman province in the 1st century BC, Roman soldiers try to follow the Nile upstream. They are stopped by the Sudd, a huge, reedy swamp.

The Egyptians reach Punt where they load up their ships with riches. They bring back incense and myrrh trees which are needed for Queen Hatshepsut's temple.

PUNT?

ANCIENT CHINESE EXPLORERS

ABOUT 2,000 YEARS AGO the ancient Romans and the Chinese still lived in separate worlds – their civilizations were developing in isolation. Between them lay high mountains, thick forests, and vast deserts, as well as warlike tribes who guarded their lands fiercely. Nonetheless, Chinese and Romans knew of each other's existence: silk worn by rich Romans came from China, passing through many hands on the way. It came over land, along the routes of the old Silk Road.

These routes across Central Asia were explored by a great Chinese traveller, Chang Ch'ien, in 138 BC. Ancient trade routes also led to a third centre of ancient civilization – India, the homeland of the religion of the Chinese Buddhists. Learned Buddhist monks such as Fa Hsien in AD 399 and Hsüan Tsang in AD 629, journeyed there to study and to visit the holy places where the Buddha had lived and taught.

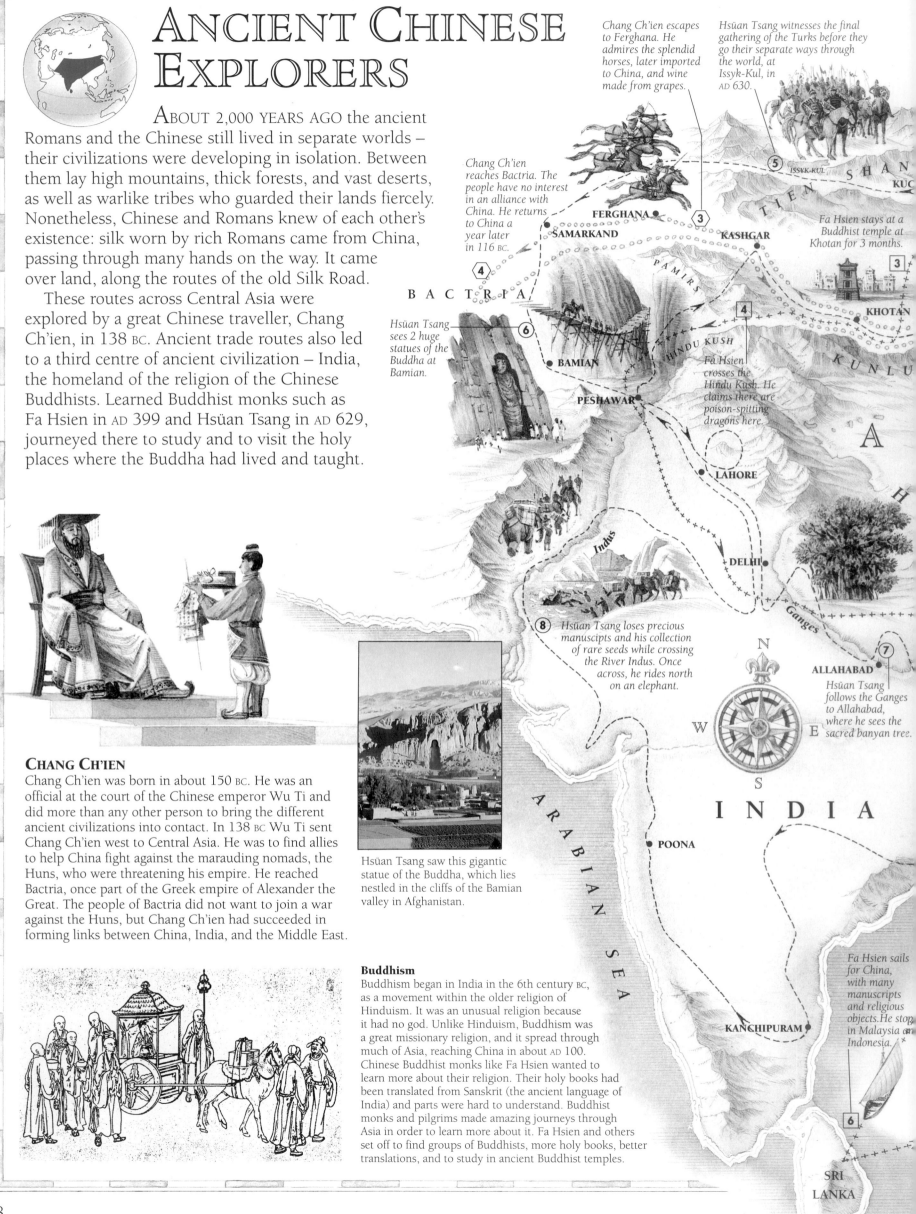

Chang Ch'ien escapes to Ferghana. He admires the splendid horses, later imported to China, and wine made from grapes.

Hsüan Tsang witnesses the final gathering of the Turks before they go their separate ways through the world, at Issyk-Kul, in AD 630.

Chang Ch'ien reaches Bactria. The people have no interest in an alliance with China. He returns to China a year later in 116 BC.

Fa Hsien stays at a Buddhist temple at Khotan for 3 months.

Hsüan Tsang sees 2 huge statues of the Buddha at Bamian.

Fa Hsien crosses the Hindu Kush. He claims there are poison-spitting dragons here.

Hsüan Tsang loses precious manuscripts and his collection of rare seeds while crossing the River Indus. Once across, he rides north on an elephant.

Hsüan Tsang follows the Ganges to Allahabad, where he sees the sacred banyan tree.

Fa Hsien sails for China, with many manuscripts and religious objects. He stops in Malaysia and Indonesia.

FERGHANA · SAMARKAND · KASHGAR · KHOTAN · BACTRIA · BAMIAN · PESHAWAR · LAHORE · DELHI · ALLAHABAD · POONA · KANCHIPURAM · TIEN SHAN · KUC · PAMIRS · HINDU KUSH · KUNLU · ISSYK-KUL · Indus · Ganges · ARABIAN SEA · INDIA · SRI LANKA

Hsüan Tsang saw this gigantic statue of the Buddha, which lies nestled in the cliffs of the Bamian valley in Afghanistan.

CHANG CH'IEN

Chang Ch'ien was born in about 150 BC. He was an official at the court of the Chinese emperor Wu Ti and did more than any other person to bring the different ancient civilizations into contact. In 138 BC Wu Ti sent Chang Ch'ien west to Central Asia. He was to find allies to help China fight against the marauding nomads, the Huns, who were threatening his empire. He reached Bactria, once part of the Greek empire of Alexander the Great. The people of Bactria did not want to join a war against the Huns, but Chang Ch'ien had succeeded in forming links between China, India, and the Middle East.

Buddhism

Buddhism began in India in the 6th century BC, as a movement within the older religion of Hinduism. It was an unusual religion because it had no god. Unlike Hinduism, Buddhism was a great missionary religion, and it spread through much of Asia, reaching China in about AD 100. Chinese Buddhist monks like Fa Hsien wanted to learn more about their religion. Their holy books had been translated from Sanskrit (the ancient language of India) and parts were hard to understand. Buddhist monks and pilgrims made amazing journeys through Asia in order to learn more about it. Fa Hsien and others set off to find groups of Buddhists, more holy books, better translations, and to study in ancient Buddhist temples.

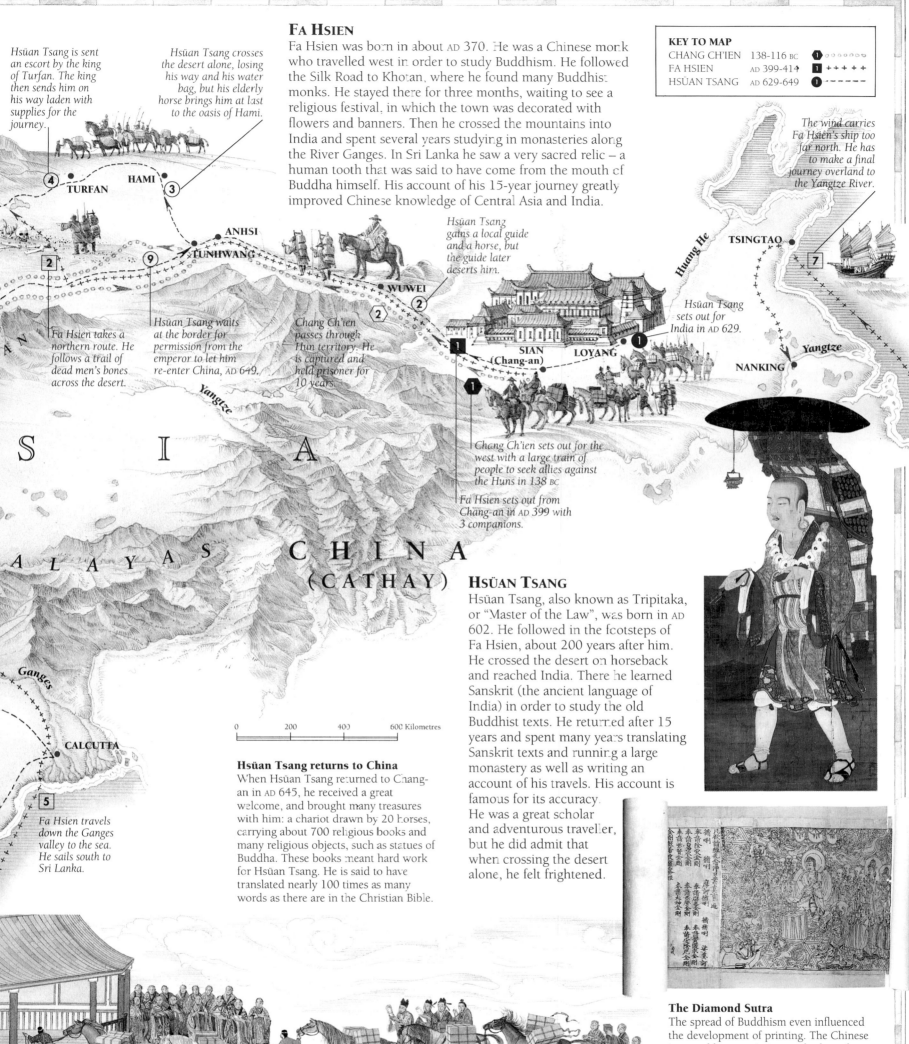

Fa Hsien

Fa Hsien was born in about AD 370. He was a Chinese monk who travelled west in order to study Buddhism. He followed the Silk Road to Khotan, where he found many Buddhist monks. He stayed there for three months, waiting to see a religious festival, in which the town was decorated with flowers and banners. Then he crossed the mountains into India and spent several years studying in monasteries along the River Ganges. In Sri Lanka he saw a very sacred relic – a human tooth that was said to have come from the mouth of Buddha himself. His account of his 15-year journey greatly improved Chinese knowledge of Central Asia and India.

KEY TO MAP

CHANG CH'IEN	138-116 BC	① ∘∘∘∘∘
FA HSIEN	AD 399-414	① +++++
HSÜAN TSANG	AD 629-649	① - - - - -

Hsüan Tsang is sent an escort by the king of Turfan. The king then sends him on his way laden with supplies for the journey.

Hsüan Tsang crosses the desert alone, losing his way and his water bag, but his elderly horse brings him at last to the oasis of Hami.

The wind carries Fa Hsien's ship too far north. He has to make a final journey overland to the Yangtze River.

Hsüan Tsang gains a local guide and a horse, but the guide later deserts him.

Hsüan Tsang sets out for India in AD 629.

Fa Hsien takes a northern route. He follows a trail of dead men's bones across the desert.

Hsüan Tsang waits at the border for permission from the emperor to let him re-enter China, AD 649.

Chang Ch'ien passes through Hun territory. He is captured and held prisoner for 10 years.

Chang Ch'ien sets out for the west with a large train of people to seek allies against the Huns in 138 BC

Fa Hsien sets out from Chang-an in AD 399 with 3 companions.

Fa Hsien travels down the Ganges valley to the sea. He sails south to Sri Lanka.

Hsüan Tsang returns to China

When Hsüan Tsang returned to Chang-an in AD 645, he received a great welcome, and brought many treasures with him: a chariot drawn by 20 horses, carrying about 700 religious books and many religious objects, such as statues of Buddha. These books meant hard work for Hsüan Tsang. He is said to have translated nearly 100 times as many words as there are in the Christian Bible.

Hsüan Tsang

Hsüan Tsang, also known as Tripitaka, or "Master of the Law", was born in AD 602. He followed in the footsteps of Fa Hsien, about 200 years after him. He crossed the desert on horseback and reached India. There he learned Sanskrit (the ancient language of India) in order to study the old Buddhist texts. He returned after 15 years and spent many years translating Sanskrit texts and running a large monastery as well as writing an account of his travels. His account is famous for its accuracy. He was a great scholar and adventurous traveller, but he did admit that when crossing the desert alone, he felt frightened.

The Diamond Sutra

The spread of Buddhism even influenced the development of printing. The Chinese invented better printing methods so that more people could read sacred Buddhist texts, such as Hsüan Tsang's works. Books at that time were actually scrolls made up of sheets joined together. The "image" to be printed was carved in a wooden block, which was then covered with ink. The Diamond Sutra (above), was printed in AD 868 and is the oldest known book. It is a collection of Buddhist teachings or *sutra*.

9

VIKING VOYAGES

THE VIKINGS, MEANING "men of the creek", is the name given to the people of Scandinavia who raided the coasts of Great Britain and north-west Europe from AD 800 to 1100. But they were not only ruthless warriors, who plundered and pillaged other lands. They also travelled far from their homeland in search of new lands to trade with or settle. Their restless voyaging carried them half way around the world: west across the stormy Atlantic, south into the warm Mediterranean, and north into the freezing Arctic.

No one knows for sure why the Vikings began to venture abroad in this way. Scandinavia was a rich region, but its population was growing. Younger sons, who had no land to inherit, may have seized the chance to make their fortune by raiding foreign shores. They also became wealthy by settling new lands and escaping the taxes of their own lands.

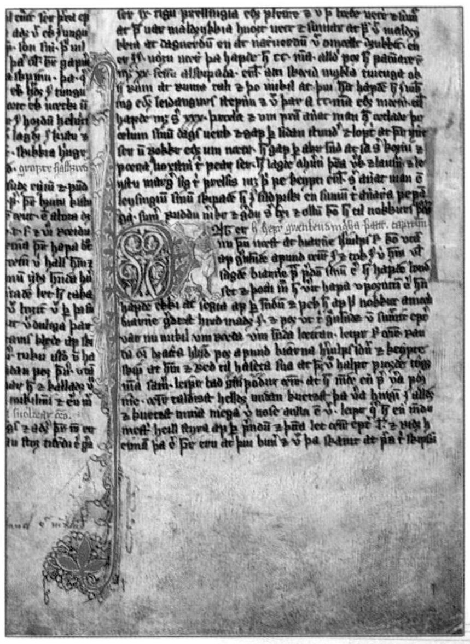

The world of the Sagas
Most of what we know about the settlement of Greenland, and the Viking voyages to North America, comes from the Norse Sagas. One of these was the *Graenlandinga Saga*, or Greenlander's Saga (left), written in the 12th century, after the Viking voyages. Although some Sagas give a history of the Norse people, they were written as stories, for entertainment, and so they are not necessarily true. For example, the Sagas tell of the one-legged inhabitants of America! Proof that the Norse Greenlanders settled in Newfoundland comes not from the Sagas, but from remains of their houses found at L'Anse aux Meadows in Newfoundland.

Remains of the Norse settlement at Brattahlid, where Eric the Red built his house.

BAFFIN ISLAND (HELLULAND)

GREENLAND

More Icelanders found a settlement near modern Godthåb. By the 15th century the climate is colder and the Norse settlements in Greenland fail.

ICELAND

REYKJAVIK

THINGVEL

GODTHÅB

Leif Eriksson names the land he first sees, Helluland ("Land of Flat Stones"). It is probably Baffin Island.

JULIANEHÅB (Brattahlid)

Eric encourages Icelanders to settle in south-west Greenland. He builds his house at Brattahlid.

Eric the Red leaves Iceland with his family and others to explore the land to the west.

NORTH AMERICA

LABRADOR (MARKLAND)

Leif comes to another land, with forests. He names it Markland, which means "Forest Land".

L'ANSE AUX MEADOWS

NEWFOUNDLAND

A settlement is made in Newfoundland: a group of huts called "Leif's Houses".

Thingvellir in Iceland, the site of an early form of Viking parliament.

VINLAND?

ATLANTIC OCEAN

Leif's men discover Vinland ("Wine-land"), where wild grapes grow. Later settlers fight local people whom they call skraelings (meaning "savage wretches").

KEY TO MAP
Viking routes 800–1100 . . . .

The true discovery of America

Norsemen and women visited North America nearly 500 years before Columbus' famous voyage in the 1490s. Bjarni Herjulfsson, whose ship had been blown off course between Iceland and Greenland, brought information about land farther west to Eric the Red. Eric's son, Leif Eriksson, led an expedition to explore the land. The painting below shows Leif Eriksson catching sight of Helluland. One man, travelling farther south, reported an area of fertile land where there were vines of wild grapes growing. Because of this Leif named this land Vinland or Wine-land. All of this suggests that the Norsemen sailed a long way south, to the north-east states of America.

Finding the way

The Norsemen who sailed across the Atlantic could tell their position roughly by the stars. They had neither charts nor instruments to help them navigate, but they did have a kind of compass, called a bearing dial (left). One of the notches on the dial indicates South. At noon, this notch lines up with a point on the horizon directly below the sun. The navigator set the course with the pointer.

Eric the Red

In the 980s, a Norse chieftain called Eric the Red, who had settled in Iceland, became an outlaw after killing a man in a quarrel. Eric had heard tales of lands to the west, and so he sailed there. The climate was milder then, and Eric decided to start a settlement in this new land. Finding summer grass growing near the shore, he called the place "Greenland", hoping that this name would attract more people to settle there. In fact, Greenland is colder and icier than Iceland, which has volcanoes and hot springs. In spite of this, Eric's colony survived and slowly grew.

The Swedish Viking, Floki (known as Raven-Floki), sails west, guided by ravens that he has released. He reaches the east coast of Iceland where he builds a house.

Norsemen find the Faroe Islands and Iceland in about AD 800, perhaps by following the flight of birds.

0   200   400   600   800 Kilometres

A Norse ship

The Vikings could not have travelled so far without very good ships. The longships they used on raids were fast and sleek, powered by sail or oars. But the Vikings used wide-bellied ships when they went on trading voyages or to settle new land. These ships were shorter and wider than the longships, with more room for passengers and cargo. They depended mainly on a large square sail, but they could also be rowed. The mast and sail could be used to make a roof, like a tent, over the ship when it was moored. The *knorr* was the largest type of cargo ship, measuring up to 16 m long and 4-5 m wide.

Following the rivers

The Viking traders from Sweden and Norway, who made long journeys across Russia, followed the rivers inland as far as they could. Their boats were light and shallow so that they could be taken upriver. When they had to cross from one river to another, or find a way around a waterfall, they could carry or pull the boats overland, as shown in the 16th-century woodcut (left).

FAROE ISLANDS

TRONDHEIM

SHETLAND ISLANDS

BERGEN

OSLO

KAUPANG

N O R W A Y

S W E D E N

BALTIC SEA

B R I T I S H   I S L E S

E U R O P E

The travels of the Vikings in Europe

Although the Vikings discovered new lands in the west, across the Atlantic, they travelled even farther to the east, across Europe and into Asia. The Danes settled in north-east England and raided the coasts of Italy and North Africa. The Swedes established trade routes that reached from the Baltic to the Caspian Sea and the Black Sea. From the Black Sea they sailed to Constantinople. From the Caspian, they followed the Silk Road to China. The Norwegians took over the Northern Isles of Scotland and founded cities such as Dublin, Cork, and Waterford in Ireland. Other Norse folk bought land from the king of France and settled in what became Normandy (The name "Normans" comes from "Northmen" or "Norsemen".)

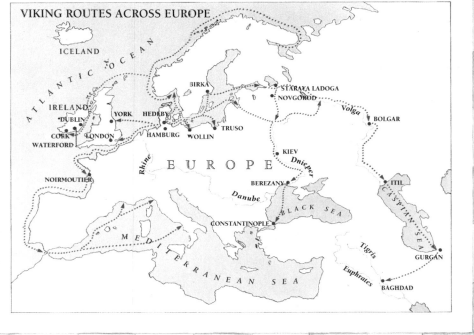

VIKING ROUTES ACROSS EUROPE

ICELAND

ATLANTIC OCEAN

IRELAND
DUBLIN
CORK
WATERFORD
YORK
LONDON
HEDEBY
HAMBURG
WOLLIN
BIRKA
TRUSO
STARAYA LADOGA
NOVGOROD
KIEV
BEREZANY
Volga
BOLGAR
ITIL
Rhine
Danube
Dnieper
E U R O P E
CASPIAN SEA
NOIRMOUTIER
CONSTANTINOPLE
BLACK SEA
MEDITERRANEAN SEA
Tigris
Euphrates
GURGAN
BAGHDAD

MUSLIM TRAVELLERS

THE GREAT RELIGION of Islam, founded in the seventh century spread as far as Spain and India in only 200 years. In spite of their many different nationalities, the followers of Islam, called Muslims, share many traditions, including the language and knowledge of the Arabs (the first followers of Islam). Educated Muslims, such as Ibn Battuta, travelled through this huge region, and found a sympathetic welcome in many places. The Arabs were great travellers and seekers of knowledge. Besides those who travelled as merchants, all Muslims tried to visit the holy city of Mecca. From the ninth century onwards, many Muslims left records of what they had seen and what they had done, not only in Islamic countries but beyond. Their accounts often contained doubtful stories, but they were also full of fascinating facts.

Mecca
The desert city of Mecca in Arabia, where Mohammed, the founder of Islam, was born in AD 570 (in the Christian calendar). It is the holiest city in Islam. When they pray, Muslims face Mecca. In the centre of the city is the *Ka'ba*, meaning cube, a sacred shrine older than Islam. It is supposed to have been built by the prophet Abraham, also revered by the Jews as the founder of their religion, and is believed to be a place where heavenly power directly touches the Earth.

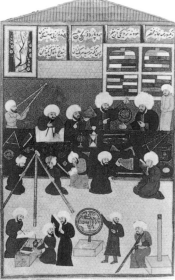

Muslim scholars
Scientific knowledge was advanced in Islam in the 12th century. While Christians still believed that the Earth was flat, Muslim scholars knew it is round. Muslim scholars (above) wrote books, built observatories and founded many centres of learning. The Arabs were also good navigators. The astrolabe (right) was an early navigational aid, and probably an Arab invention.

Al Idrisi
The famous Arab geographer Al Idrisi was born in North Africa in about 1100. He travelled through much of Europe and the Near East and worked for many years for Roger II, King of Sicily. He produced a map of the world (left), a globe of the Earth and a huge guide for travellers. The map even shows a possible source of the Nile, which isn't far from the true source.

Ibn Battuta leaves Tangier to visit the holy cities of Arabia, 1325.

Ibn Battuta sets out on his last journey, joining a caravan from Fez, 1352.

Ibn Battuta rejoins his southward route at Sijilmassa, where he claims he encounters a snowstorm. He crosses the Atlas Mountains and reaches Fez, Sept 1353.

Ibn Battuta weds his first of many wives in Tripoli.

Ibn Battuta passes through Taghaza, a salt village; even the homes of the salt workers are made of rock salt, with camel-skin roofs.

Ibn Battuta's party return through the Hoggar Mountains. They stop at an oasis on the other side of the mountains.

Ibn Battuta is in unknown territory at Walata, so he hires a guide. Along the route he notices many ancient baobab trees.

Ibn Battuta spends 6 months in Timbuktu, a centre of trade, with a fine, mud-walled mosque. He then joins a caravan to Takedda.

Ibn Battuta mistakes the great River Niger for the Nile, as did many other early travellers. He is astonished by his first sight of water horses (hippos).

MEDITERRANEAN

TANGIER — FEZ — ATLAS MOUNTAINS — MARRAKESH — SIJILMASSA — TRIPOLI — TAGHAZA — TUAT OASIS — SAHARA DE — HOGGAR MOUNTAINS — TAKEDDA — Senegal — WALATA — TIMBUKTU — GAO — Niger — MALI — Niger

ATLANTIC OCEAN

KEY TO MAP		
IBN BATTUTA		
Travels	1324-32	●·········
Travels	1352-53	■‑ ‑ ‑ ‑

IBN BATTUTA

Ibn Battuta was born in Tangier, on the coast of North Africa. He spent most of his life travelling or living in distant places and was the greatest of all Muslim travellers. Altogether he travelled over 100,000 km. We know little about him except what we learn from his *Travels*, which he dictated after his return. Some tales, such as his claim that he visited Christian Constantinople and saw 12,000 bishops in the cathedral, are rather hard to believe. Some stories may have been put in by someone else, perhaps the person who wrote down his words.

Ibn Battuta 1304-1377

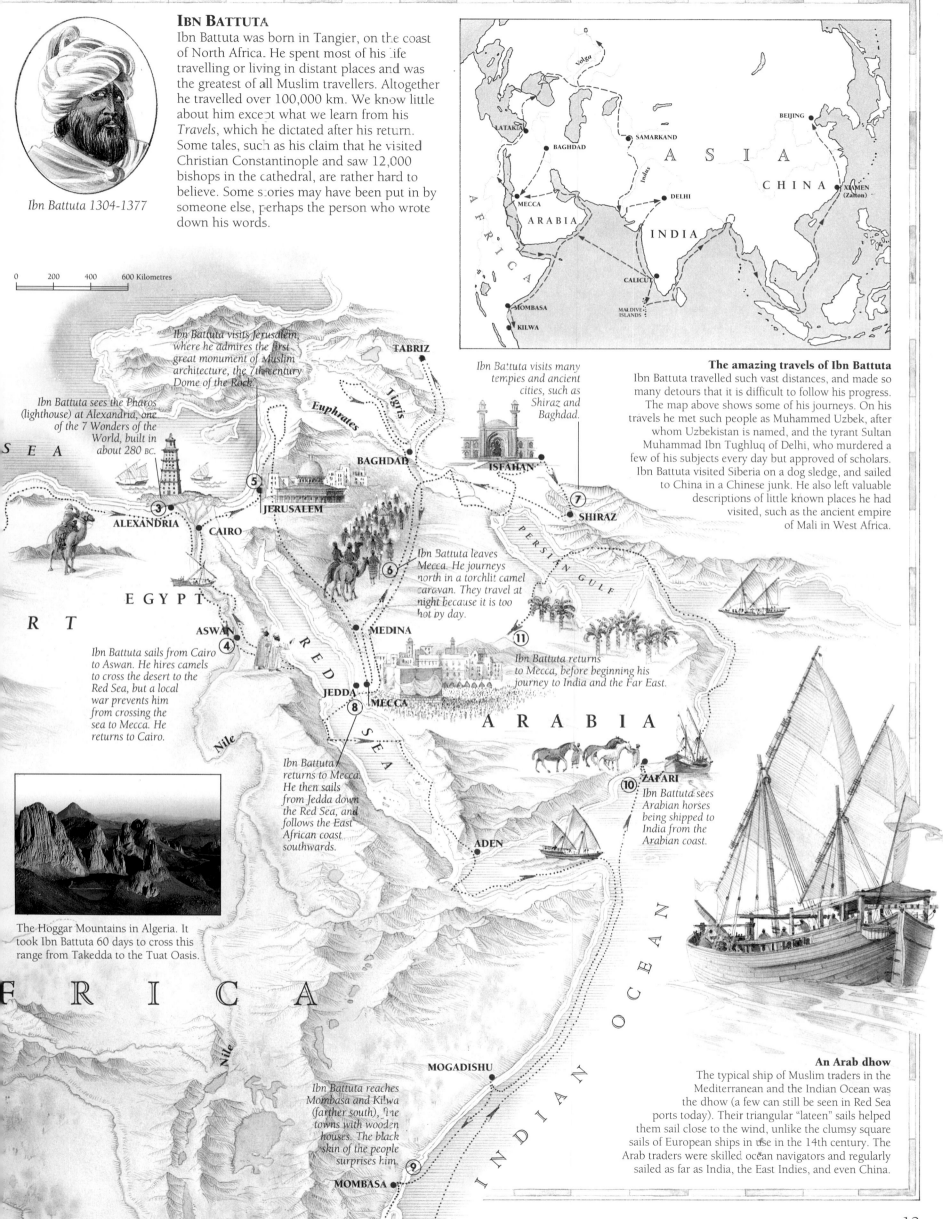

The amazing travels of Ibn Battuta

Ibn Battuta travelled such vast distances, and made so many detours that it is difficult to follow his progress. The map above shows some of his journeys. On his travels he met such people as Muhammed Uzbek, after whom Uzbekistan is named, and the tyrant Sultan Muhammad Ibn Tughluq of Delhi, who murdered a few of his subjects every day but approved of scholars. Ibn Battuta visited Siberia on a dog sledge, and sailed to China in a Chinese junk. He also left valuable descriptions of little known places he had visited, such as the ancient empire of Mali in West Africa.

Ibn Battuta visits Jerusalem, where he admires the first great monument of Muslim architecture, the 7th century Dome of the Rock.

Ibn Battuta sees the Pharos (lighthouse) at Alexandria, one of the 7 Wonders of the World, built in about 280 BC.

Ibn Battuta visits many temples and ancient cities, such as Shiraz and Baghdad.

Ibn Battuta leaves Mecca. He journeys north in a torchlit camel caravan. They travel at night because it is too hot by day.

Ibn Battuta sails from Cairo to Aswan. He hires camels to cross the desert to the Red Sea, but a local war prevents him from crossing the sea to Mecca. He returns to Cairo.

Ibn Battuta returns to Mecca, before beginning his journey to India and the Far East.

Ibn Battuta returns to Mecca. He then sails from Jedda down the Red Sea, and follows the East African coast southwards.

Ibn Battuta sees Arabian horses being shipped to India from the Arabian coast.

The Hoggar Mountains in Algeria. It took Ibn Battuta 60 days to cross this range from Takedda to the Tuat Oasis.

Ibn Battuta reaches Mombasa and Kilwa (farther south), fine towns with wooden houses. The black skin of the people surprises him.

An Arab dhow

The typical ship of Muslim traders in the Mediterranean and the Indian Ocean was the dhow (a few can still be seen in Red Sea ports today). Their triangular "lateen" sails helped them sail close to the wind, unlike the clumsy square sails of European ships in use in the 14th century. The Arab traders were skilled ocean navigators and regularly sailed as far as India, the East Indies, and even China.

13

TRAVEL FOR TRADE

THE SPIRIT OF DISCOVERY is an urge that has taken explorers throughout history on great voyages. But when this spirit is combined with the urge to make money, it becomes even more powerful, driving trader-explorers to the most distant corners of the Earth. The sailors of the Mediterranean were among the first international traders and explorers. Transport by sea has always been quick and, in sheltered waters, relatively easy. However, until the 15th century, ocean routes from the Middle East to Africa and Southeast Asia were difficult, dangerous, or unknown. So traders often used overland routes to these areas. The expense of overland transport meant that only the most valuable goods were worth trading. From the East came the finest silk, jade, porcelain, and spices. Gold from Africa was carried across the shifting sands of the Sahara. And in depot cities, such as Alexandria in Egypt, the merchants exchanged travellers' tales as they met to buy, sell, and barter.

Barter, gold, and money

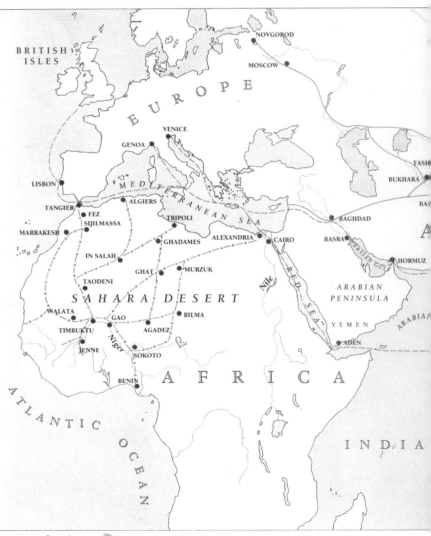

Early traders did not carry money when they travelled. They used barter – swapping or exchanging goods. Traders from a desert civilization skilled in metalwork, for example, might visit a forest community and barter axe-heads for timber. In the desert, timber is more valuable; in the forest people need axes but have surplus trees. Eventually, gold replaced barter because traders could exchange it for anything.

The salt trade

Today we sprinkle salt so freely that it is difficult to imagine a time when it was so precious that people were paid in it. Yet this is the origin of the word "salary". Salt can be made by evaporating seawater, but it also occurs as a mineral deposit close to the Earth's surface, especially in hot climates, as in the Sahara Desert. The photograph (left) shows salt crystallizing in the sun. As the water evaporates, crystals of salt remain. Salt is a vital part of the diet in warm areas where sweating causes salt loss, and salting is an important method of preserving food. Salt traders transported it from the coasts, and inland deposits, to areas where it was scarce and valuable. Even today the salt trade is vital to the economy of desert peoples.

Salt routes

Camel trains carried huge quantities of salt from its sources in and around the Sahara Desert to the Mediterranean for shipment to Europe. The salt trade was largely controlled by nomadic desert people, who bartered their product with those who lived in desert oases. The Greek historian, Herodotus (about 485-425 BC) describes the salt trade routes in the Sahara Desert and the routes linking some of the desert oases.

The lure of gold

The beauty of gold has made this metal extremely valuable since the earliest times. Until the mid-14th century, most of the world's gold came from West Africa, in the form of granules or dust. Muslim traders and adventurers took caravans carrying luxury goods and salt across the Sahara to the gold-mining areas. They returned with gold and slaves for sale in the Middle East and Europe. Trade with the Far East increased the demand for gold, which was used to pay for Chinese silk and other luxuries.

Ports and entrepôts

Trade goods often changed hands many times along the route, and might be offloaded and stored at entrepôts (temporary depots and trading posts) while awaiting shipment. Hormuz in Iran (below) was a fortified trading post on the Persian Gulf, visited by Marco Polo in the 13th century.

ORMVS.

The silk trade

Silk production began in northern China more than 4,500 years ago. For 2,000 years the process was a closely guarded secret. Silk threads come from a cocoon – a coat that the silkworm spins around itself for protection while it grows into a moth. To make silk fabric, workers unwind the threads from the cocoon, twist them together into thread and weave the threads on a loom. Silk is valuable because it makes very strong, beautiful cloth, and because more than 2,500 cocoons must be unwound by hand to make just 500 g of yarn.

The Silk Road

Traders and their animals travelled in groups, called caravans. They rested and refreshed themselves along the route at a series of *caravanserais*, or inns (above). Merchants leading rows of snorting, heavily-laden camels brought silk to the Middle East and Europe along the Silk Road. This ancient road was actually several different routes that skirted the deserts and mountains on the way through India and Central Asia. Western traders explored the route as early as the first century AD. In the second century the geographer Ptolemy described a stone tower in the Pamir mountains where traders met to barter.

KEY TO MAP

Map shows general trade routes in the 10th to 14th centuries.

Main silk route	———
Main gold and salt route	–•–•–•–
Main spice route	– – – –

Jade and porcelain

Western traders carrying gold along the Silk Road often returned with porcelain, and carvings made of jade – a hard green gemstone. Beautiful jade carvings, such as the horse (left) fetched high prices even in China, where for many centuries jade was the most precious substance known. The Chinese invented porcelain, a delicate, semi-transparent pottery, in the eighth century. People paid high prices for Chinese porcelain in fashionable European cities.

The spice trade

When the Queen of Sheba visited the wealthy King Solomon, the Bible reports that she took "…twenty talents of gold, and of spices very great store, and precious stones". Thousands of years ago people of the Middle East valued spices as highly as gold. In Europe, spices were important for flavouring meat that had been preserved in salt for months. Most of the spices used grew wild in the Far East, but even in biblical times they were cultivated as crops for sale. Pepper became so precious that it was, at times, used as money in the West as well as the East. Some people even paid their taxes with peppercorns.

Spice routes

Spices travelled to the West by a number of different routes. The Queen of Sheba's spices probably went by Chinese junk (above) from Southeast Asia, via the Bay of Bengal, and then by Arab dhow across the Arabian Sea. The ships landed on the Hadhramaut coast of what is now Yemen, on the Arabian Peninsula. From there, traders took the precious cargo overland. Other sea routes continued up the Red Sea to Alexandria, or hugged the coast of India, ending at Hormuz at the mouth of the Persian Gulf. All this changed in the final years of the 15th century when the Portuguese found a sea route from Europe around Africa to the Spice Islands.

Nutmeg

Nutmeg is the kernel of a fruit that grows in the Spice Islands of Southeast Asia. The Dutch monopolized trade in this valuable spice (left) when they gained control of the islands from the Portuguese in the 17th century.

Pepper

Peppercorns grow wild on a vine in the monsoon forests of India's southwest coast. Pepper and a related plant were farmed all over southern Asia more than 2,000 years ago.

Cinnamon

At one time cinnamon (left) was more valuable than gold. Cinnamon comes from the bark of the cinnamon tree, which grows in Sri Lanka, the West Indies, and Brazil.

Cloves

The unopened buds of a tropical tree (left) provide cloves. The tree once grew all over the East Indies, but to make the spice more expensive the Dutch uprooted many clove trees.

MARCO POLO IN CHINA

THE GREATEST LUXURIES in medieval Europe – spices and silks – came from the Far East. Yet although the East had been trading with the West for centuries, the two civilizations knew little about one another. Asian merchants took goods from the Far East as far as the Persian Gulf or the Black Sea, following an overland route along the old Silk Road, or a sea route around the coasts of southern Asia. Goods were then sent to ports on the Mediterranean, where European merchants bought them. Traders were forced to use these roundabout routes because the most direct path, across Central Asia, was blocked by Islamic countries, who would not allow free travel across their land. This changed in the 13th century when the Mongols, led by Genghis Khan, conquered a huge area stretching from eastern Europe to China, bringing peace to the region. At last, merchants could travel freely across Asia. The Italian Polo brothers were among the first Europeans to set off, from Venice, in 1260.

The Polos travel east
In the 13th century, Venice was the richest city in Europe, thanks to its trading links with the East. Once the Mongols had opened trade routes, Venetian merchants set out for Cathay (modern China) for the first time. The brothers Niccolo and Maffeo Polo, set out from Venice in 1260 and reached the Mongol capital of Cambaluc (modern Beijing) where the Mongol emperor, Kublai Khan, welcomed them.

Marco Polo 1254-1324

MARCO POLO
In 1271, the Polos made a second journey to the East. This time they took Niccolo's 16-year-old son, Marco, with them. Other Europeans were now travelling across Asia, but Marco's journey was unique because he stayed in Kublai Khan's empire for 20 years. During this time he travelled widely in the vast Mongol Empire. On his return to Europe he wrote a splendid book describing all that he had seen.

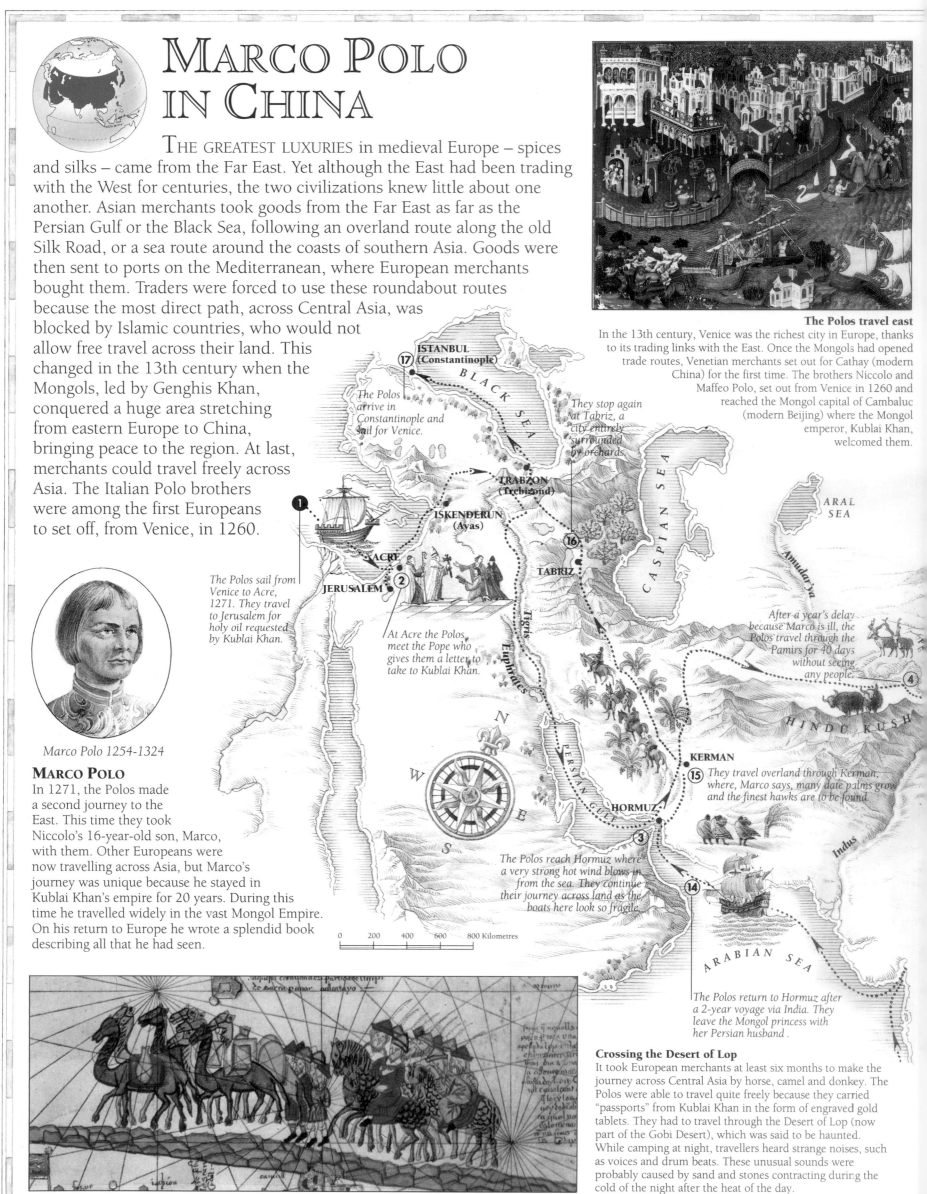

ISTANBUL (Constantinople)

The Polos arrive in Constantinople and sail for Venice.

BLACK SEA

They stop again at Tabriz, a city entirely surrounded by orchards.

TRABZON (Trebizond)

ISKENDERUN (Ayas)

ACRE

JERUSALEM

The Polos sail from Venice to Acre, 1271. They travel to Jerusalem for holy oil requested by Kublai Khan.

At Acre the Polos meet the Pope who gives them a letter to take to Kublai Khan.

TABRIZ

CASPIAN SEA

ARAL SEA

Amudarya

After a year's delay because Marco is ill, the Polos travel through the Pamirs for 40 days without seeing any people.

HINDU KUSH

Tigris

Euphrates

PERSIAN GULF

KERMAN

They travel overland through Kerman, where, Marco says, many date palms grow and the finest hawks are to be found.

Indus

HORMUZ

The Polos reach Hormuz where a very strong hot wind blows in from the sea. They continue their journey across land as the boats here look so fragile.

0   200   400   600   800 Kilometres

ARABIAN SEA

The Polos return to Hormuz after a 2-year voyage via India. They leave the Mongol princess with her Persian husband.

Crossing the Desert of Lop
It took European merchants at least six months to make the journey across Central Asia by horse, camel and donkey. The Polos were able to travel quite freely because they carried "passports" from Kublai Khan in the form of engraved gold tablets. They had to travel through the Desert of Lop (now part of the Gobi Desert), which was said to be haunted. While camping at night, travellers heard strange noises, such as voices and drum beats. These unusual sounds were probably caused by sand and stones contracting during the cold of the night after the heat of the day.

At the Great Khan's palace

Kublai Khan first received the Polos at his magnificent summer palace in Shangdu. He welcomed them warmly, although he was disappointed to find that they had come alone. He had hoped they would bring Christian priests who might perform magic tricks. Niccolo Polo introduced Marco as: "my son and your servant". Marco then worked for Kublai Khan for the next 20 years. He became a great admirer of Kublai, who was a very intelligent and civilized man, in spite of being the grandson of the infamous conqueror, Genghis Khan.

According to Marco Polo it took a month to cross the Gobi Desert. He described it as "composed of hills and valleys of sand", where "not a thing to eat is to be found."

Cambaluc

Cambaluc was Kublai Khan's capital in China. It replaced the old Mongol capital of Karakorum. A huge white wall, about 30 km long, surrounded the city. Marco Polo described Cambaluc as a rich and busy place, with streets so wide and straight that you could see from one side of the city to the other. The streets divided the city up like lines on a chess board, and each square contained a fine house with courtyards and gardens.

The Great Wall of China was built to protect China from invasion, but it was not enough to keep the powerful Mongol armies out. At the time of Marco Polo's travels, the Mongol emperor ruled the land on both sides of it.

The Polos cross the desert. At night they put up signs pointing in the direction they are going, so that they don't get lost the next day.

The Polos spend a year in Campichu. Marco describes it as a large splendid city filled with gold statues. Nearby they come across Mongol herdsmen.

The Polos reach Kublai Khan's summer palace at Shangdu, May 1275. The journey has taken 3 1/2 years.

Marco stays at Kublai Khan's winter palace in Cambaluc. The Khan sends him to explore his empire.

Marco is surprised to see that the Chinese use paper money, which is unknown in Europe.

Marco crosses a wide river. He sees ginger, silk, bamboo and many birds in the countryside nearby.

Marco visits the important Chinese city of Kinsai. He says it has 12,000 bridges. This kind of exaggeration later gains him the nickname "Marco Millions".

Marco heads south. He passes many fortified villages and sees lions, tigers and bears. He travels farther west, perhaps even as far as Burma.

The Polos set sail in a fleet of Chinese junks, Jan 1292. The Khan asks them to accompany a Mongol princess, who is to marry a Persian chieftain.

Map labels:
KARAKORUM · SHANGDU · BEIJING (Cambaluc) · KASHI (Kashgar) · KHOTAN · GOBI DESERT (DESERT OF LOP) · CAMPICHU · SIAN · CHANGZHOU · HANGZHOU (Kinsai) · FUZHOU · CHENGDU (Sin-din-fu) · XIAMEN (Zaiton) · CHINA (CATHAY) · KUNMING (Yachi) · BHAMO · JAPAN (CIPANGU) · HIMALAYAS · INDIA · Ganges · Yangtze · Huang He · Great Wall of China · BAY OF BENGAL · SOUTH CHINA SEA · Irrawaddy

Tales of monsters

Europeans in the Middle Ages knew only legends about other continents. They believed travellers' tales of monsters and strange-looking people, such as the wolf-man and the man with no head (left). Marco Polo was more truthful than most, but even he reported people with thick tails and dog's heads.

Marco tells of his travels

In 1298, soon after he returned home, Marco Polo was captured by the Genoese who were at war with Venice. While in prison, he told the story of his travels to a fellow prisoner, a man named Rustichello, who wrote it down in French. Rustichello was the author of romantic tales, and some of the "tall stories" in Marco Polo's account of his travels may have been put in by Rustichello to make the story more interesting.

THE POLYNESIANS

WHEN THE EUROPEANS began to explore the Pacific and its islands, about 200 years ago, they were amazed to find that people living thousands of miles apart spoke almost the same language. This suggested that they had the same ancestors. But where had those ancestors come from? And how did they come to settle in a triangle of tiny islands scattered across the Pacific – from Hawaii in the north to New Zealand in the south, and Easter Island a long way to the east?

The Polynesians, as the people of this region are called, have no written history. But there are some clues to their origins. Most experts today believe that the Polynesians' ancestors came from Indonesia and Malaysia, between 1,000 and 3,000 years ago. There are several reasons for this: the Polynesian language is like Malay, some of the animals they kept were from south-east Asia, and most of the crops grown by Polynesians in the 18th century were Asian types. The Maori, who arrived in New Zealand after a long canoe journey across the Pacific, are Polynesians too.

Lapita ware

The ancestors of the Polynesians made a type of patterned pottery, called Lapita ware. Broken pieces, nearly 2,000 years old, have been found in some Pacific islands, together with the tools used to make them. Since archaeologists can tell roughly when these pieces were made, they can trace the movements of the Lapita group of Polynesians from one group of islands to another.

KEY TO MAP

Sites where Lapita pottery was found
Sites where sweet potatoes were found
Kon-Tiki expedition 1947

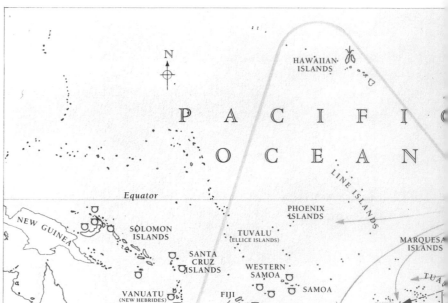

Navigation

The ancestors of the Polynesians found some of the islands where they settled by accident. However, they were skilled navigators as well as ship-builders. They had no maps or instruments, but they knew the meaning of wind changes and wave patterns, and they could follow a course by the sun and stars. Each island had its "on top" star. For example, the "on top" star for Tahiti was Sirius. When Sirius was overhead, Polynesian navigators knew they were in the latitude of Tahiti.

Navigational stick chart

Polynesians trained their navigators using a stick chart (below), made from palm sticks tied together with coconut fibre. The framework of sticks represented thousands of kilometres of sea, and the shells threaded on to the sticks marked the position of islands. It is not known when these charts were introduced, but the early Polynesian explorers probably didn't have them. They may have followed the direction of migrating birds towards land.

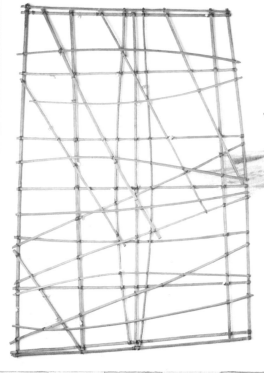

Ocean-going canoes

The Polynesians made several types of canoe for ocean sailing. Some were single-hulled canoes, made from tree-trunks, or from boards sewn together with fibre. Others, such as the Hawaiian double canoe (above), had two hulls joined together, like a catamaran. The canoes had sails as well as paddles, and some were large enough to carry men, women and children, food supplies, and weapons. When Captain Cook measured a Maori canoe in New Zealand in 1770, he found that it was one metre longer than the ship in which he was sailing around the world.

Bird prow

Ornaments such as this carved frigate bird prow decorated Polynesian canoes. Masters of flight, frigate birds swoop down to the surface to snatch their prey from the water.

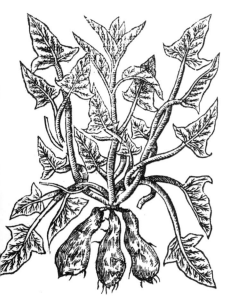

The sweet potato: another mystery

Although the sweet potato comes from tropical America, it grows in New Zealand, Hawaii and other Polynesian islands. So how did it get to these places? Some experts believe that the presence of sweet potatoes in the Polynesian islands proves that the early settlers came not from Asia, but from South America, probably Peru. But the question remains: could the ancient Peruvians have sailed so far? Thor Heyerdahl, a Norwegian scholar and explorer, proved that they could. In 1947 he sailed 6,900 km, from Peru to the Tuamotu Archipelago, in a raft modelled on ancient Peruvian craft.

The *Kon-Tiki* expedition

This raft, built in 1947 by Thor Heyerdahl, was named after the legendary Peruvian sun-god, Kon-Tiki, who was believed to have migrated from Peru to the Pacific Islands about 1,500 years ago. Heyerdahl's raft was modelled on traditional ancient Peruvian rafts. The Kon-Tiki was 13.7 m long and 5.5 m wide, and was made of balsawood logs, supporting a bamboo deck and hut. Carried by the current, Thor Heyerdahl and his crew sailed the *Kon-Tiki* from the coast of Peru to the Tuamotus – a distance of nearly 6,900 km. The journey lasted 101 days and the raft was wrecked off the Tuamotu Archipelago. However, he had proved that the Peruvians could have sailed to Polynesia and become the first settlers.

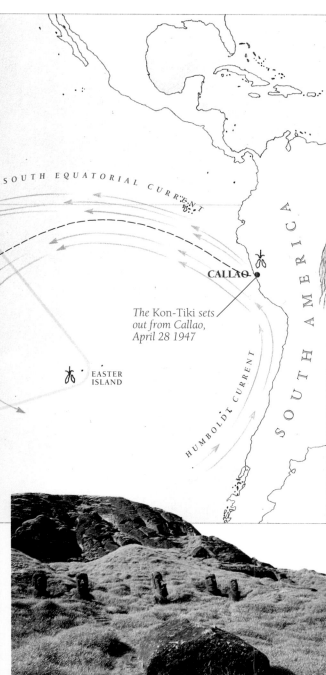

The Kon-Tiki sets out from Callao, April 28 1947

The Maori

According to tradition, the Maori sailed from the Marquesas to New Zealand. The most recent immigrants arrived in about 1350, in what Maori legend refers to as a "great fleet". They lived in tribes known as *iwi*, each with its own land and villages. Some *iwi* were named after canoes in the "great fleet". Many Polynesians practised tattooing, but it was the Maori who made it into a fine art. A Maori chief, such as the man shown above, wore the traditional headdress of feathers, and the tattoos of his tribe.

Maori fortification

The engraving above shows a Maori settlement on Mount Egmont, New Zealand. The Maori, who were a warlike people, often built fortified villages on clifftops, so that they could see their enemies approaching. They also kept their war canoes at the ready in case they were challenged. Although the Maori fought each other, in times of peace different tribes would get together for feasts, with dancing, wrestling, and games.

Easter Island

On Easter Sunday, 1722, a Dutch captain, Jacob Roggeveen, discovered a small island in the eastern Pacific. Easter Island, as the Dutch named it, had been settled around AD 400. This grassy island, measuring only 38 km across at its widest point, is more than 1,600 km from the nearest Pacific island and 3,218 km from the mainland of Chile. Because they were so far away from any other land, the people of Easter Island believed they were the only people on Earth. The Dutch found that the islanders had their own distinctive culture: they were the only Polynesians who had developed a form of writing, using picture symbols, and they were skilled stone carvers.

Guardians of Easter Island

When Roggeveen arrived at Easter Island in 1722, he discovered hundreds of gigantic stone statues around the coast. These carved figures (left), called *Moai*, are made of soft volcanic stone, and some have round "topknots" or crowns made of a different, reddish stone. The figures, which numbered about 600, were sometimes as tall as 20 m and weighed up to 45 tonnes. When they were finished, the statues were moved from the quarry and placed on a stone platform, called an *ahu*, which contained a tomb. Little is known about these mysterious statues, but it may be that the islanders saw them as guardians of the dead, or perhaps they represented the spirits of the dead themselves. Another mystery is how the islanders managed to move the statues from the quarry and position them on the platforms. They may have used a combination of trestles, sledges, ropes, and muscle power.

NAVIGATION

EARLY EUROPEAN EXPLORERS found their way in unknown seas by sailing along the coast from one landmark to the next. Once ships began sailing out of sight of land, however, they needed more reliable methods of navigation. Navigation is the art of sailing a ship by the best course, from one place on Earth to another.

Nature provided the first navigators with some help. In the Middle Ages they realized that they could work out how far north or south they were by studying the position of the Pole Star and by watching the movements of the Sun. By the 15th century – the great age of European sea exploration – navigators had developed a few instruments to guide them. For example, the compass, allowed ships to follow a set course, and the astrolabe or quadrant helped calculate position. Many of these tools were rough and inaccurate but, as ocean voyaging became more common, navigational instruments gradually started to improve.

Early navigation

Before navigation instruments were invented, early explorers sailed by dead reckoning, which really means intelligent guesswork. They used their knowledge of winds and currents to estimate distance and direction. In unknown waters, clues such as floating driftwood and certain types of seabird suggested that land was not far away. For example, the frigate bird was a welcome sight in tropical waters. This bird cannot land on water, so sailors knew that when they saw one, they must be nearing land.

Latitude and longitude

Today navigators can pinpoint the position of any place on Earth by referring to a set of imaginary lines round the globe, called lines of latitude and longitude. Lines of latitude circle the Earth from east to west and are measured in degrees north or south of the Equator. Lines of longitude circle the Earth from north to south and are measured in degrees east or west of a line, called the prime meridian, which runs through Greenwich in England.

Prime meridian
Line of longitude
Line of latitude
Equator

Calculating latitude and longitude

European sailors started to calculate their position in terms of latitude in the Middle Ages. By measuring the height of the Sun at noon or of the Pole Star at night, a sailor could work out his latitude. A method for calculating longitude was invented much later, in the 18th century, when the first ship's clock, the chronometer, was invented. The easiest way to work out longitude was to compare the local time at noon with the time at Greenwich, on the prime meridian. If he knew the number of hours' difference, a sailor could work out how many degrees east or west of Greenwich he was.

Sand glass

At first, time on a ship was measured by a sand glass. But this was little use on a long voyage, as it could only measure short periods of time. However, a half-minute sand glass was often used with a log line (a rope with knots tied in it at regular intervals) to measure speed. The log line was paid out behind the ship and the speed was calculated by measuring the time between knots as the line went out. A ship's speed is still given in "knots" today.

Compass

The Earth is like a giant magnet. It has two magnetic poles, which lie near the North and South Poles. Therefore a needle of magnetized iron will always point to the magnetic poles if allowed to swing freely. A magnetic compass works according to this principle. Europeans did not develop a magnetic compass until about 1200; the one shown above is a 16th-century Italian compass. Compasses were used on board ship to tell sailors in which direction they were sailing. Early compasses were not very reliable. A compass needle could be affected by other iron objects nearby, such as a ship's cannon, so voyages often went astray.

Ring for holding astrolabe

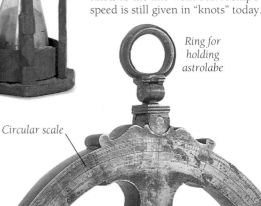

Circular scale

Rotating arm

Eyeholes

Pointer

Astrolabe

The astrolabe was a device for measuring the height of the Sun at noon. This told the navigator his latitude. Like many other navigational instruments, it was first used by astronomers, people who study the stars. An astrolabe was a disc with degrees marked on a circular scale around the edge and a rotating arm that had a small eyehole at each end. The navigator turned the arm until sunlight shone through the two eyeholes. The pointer at the end of the arm then indicated the height of the Sun in degrees above the horizon.

In line with star
Cross-piece
In line with horizon
Long arm with scale

Cross-staff

The cross-staff was an instrument used for judging latitude by measuring the height of a star. The navigator lined the cross-staff up with the horizon, then moved the sliding cross-piece until the top was in line with the star, as shown below. The long arm had a scale on it, which was marked with degrees, and the position of the cross-piece gave the height of the star in degrees above the horizon. The cross-staff was easier to use than an astrolabe, but was no use in daytime because the human eye cannot look directly at the Sun. A more complicated version, called a back-staff or English quadrant, which was invented later, solved this problem by allowing the navigator to take a reading with his back to the Sun.

Time scale disc

Moving arm

Handle

Nocturnal

The nocturnal was invented in about 1550 and was used to tell the time at night. Holding the handle at arm's length, as shown above, the navigator looked at the Pole Star through the hole in the centre of the instrument. He then moved the arm until it lined up with two other stars in the Pole Star's constellation. The arm pointed to the time on a disc in the middle of the device. The nocturnal was accurate to within about 10 minutes.

Mirrors

Moving arm

Scale

From quadrant to octant

The quadrant was probably the first instrument used by navigators to measure the height of a star in order to calculate latitude. It was a quarter-circle of brass, with a plumb line hanging straight down from the point. One of the straight edges had tiny holes at each end. The navigator looked at the star through these holes. The plumb line then showed the height of the star in degrees, which were marked along the curved edge.

The octant (left) was invented in about 1730. It was an improved version of the quadrant, with two mirrors. By moving the arm, the navigator brought the reflection of the star together with the reflection of the horizon. The arm then indicated the height of the star in degrees on the scale at the bottom.

Double mirrors

Telescope

Moving arm

Scale

Portolan chart

The earliest sailors' maps were called Portolan charts and were drawn on goatskin. The charts showed places and landmarks along a coast and were covered with direction lines and decorative compasses, known as compass "roses". These early maps were often inaccurate because their makers did not know enough geography. They were also uncertain how to show the curved surface of the Earth on a flat map. Portolan charts were used a great deal by Portuguese explorers in the 16th century. This one of the Mediterranean was made in about 1555.

Chronometer

The invention of the chronometer in the 18th century made sea navigation much easier. A chronometer is an accurate clock, which will keep nearly perfect time even when tossed about in a ship at sea for months. Most importantly, it allowed navigators to measure longitude accurately, because it could be set to keep Greenwich time. This 19th-century chronometer was used by Antarctic explorer, Ernest Shackleton, in 1914.

Sextant

The sextant (above) replaced the quadrant in the late 18th century and is still used today to measure a star's altitude. It is fitted with double mirrors and a telescope for greater accuracy and, unlike the quadrant or octant, it can measure angles greater than 90°. The one shown above was made by an English designer and was used by Captain Cook on his third voyage in 1770. Early sextants such as these had to be hand held, so ships' navigators often used them on the shore (left), rather than on board ship.

Modern navigation

In the 20th century, methods of navigation have improved enormously. In 1908, the gyroscopic compass was invented This always points to the true north and is not affected by magnetism. But the biggest breakthrough in navigational equipment was the invention of radio in around 1900. The chronometer, which was so important in the 18th century, is now unnecessary because time checks are broadcast by radio. Radio also enables ships to communicate with one another. Today, a ship anywhere in the world can also check its exact position by means of a signal from a satellite in orbit (right).

THE PORTUGUESE

THE GREAT AGE of European exploration began in the 15th century, when sailors set out for the first time on long ocean voyages. The Portuguese led the way from their little kingdom at the corner of Europe. In 1415, after centuries of fighting, they drove the Muslims out of Portugal, pursuing them as far as North Africa. Here they heard stories of gold mines hidden deep in West Africa. These stories inspired Prince Henry of Portugal, known as "the Navigator", to send his captains out on the first voyages of discovery down the African coast. In 1453, another Muslim people, the powerful Ottoman Turks, blocked the overland trade route between Europe and the Far East. Now the Portuguese had an even greater incentive for sailing south into unknown seas: the need to find a sea route to the riches of India. The first expeditions were slow and cautious. As Portuguese captains edged their way further down the coast, they set up stone pillars, called *padrões,* on the shore to mark their progress. By the end of the century, Vasco da Gama had opened up the first sea route between Europe and India.

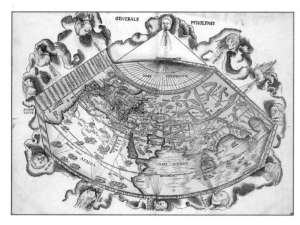

Mapping the unknown
World maps in the 15th century were based on the work of Claudius Ptolemaeus, known as Ptolemy, an ancient geographer who had been dead for more than 1,200 years! This Ptolemy map shows Europe and the Mediterranean region quite accurately, but it shows only the top half of Africa because Ptolemy had no idea how far south the continent stretched, nor if it even ended at all. The Portuguese sailors who first rounded the tip of Africa kept the reports of their voyages secret from other European nations who also wanted to find a sea route to the trade goods of the Far East.

Portuguese caravels
The daring Portuguese sea voyages of the 15th century were made possible by the development of the caravel. This was a very small ship, about 20 m long, with a crew of about 25. The first caravels were made for coastal sailing and were lateen-rigged (with triangular sails), like this one, but for ocean voyaging, square-rigged ships proved better – they were less nimble in narrow waters, but faster on the open sea.

Da Gama sails home via the Azores. (14)

Da Gama sails with 4 ships and about 150 men, bound for India, July 1497.

Dias sets out with 2 caravels and 1 storeship carrying plenty of provisions, Aug 1487.

Cão leaves Portugal to chart the African coast, June 1485.

LISBON — PORTUGAL — Tagus

AZORES

CANARY ISLANDS

CAPE BOJADOR

CAPE VERDE ISLANDS

Da Gama stops for a week in the Cape Verde Islands. (2)

Cão stops for supplies at the Portuguese trading fortress of Elmina (the Mine) (2)

ELMINA

Da Gama sets a course through the South Atlantic, sailing far from land in order to avoid the winds near the coast. (3)

Dias leaves Elmina and crosses the Gulf of Guinea to the Congo.

ATLANTIC OCEAN

DIOGO CÃO
In 1485 Diogo Cão reached Cape Cross and set up this *padrão*, which bears the coat of arms of the Portuguese King Joao II. It was a great achievement for Cão who had reached farther south down the coast of Africa than any Portuguese captain before him. Earlier captains had travelled a short distance down the coast in order to make a quick profit from trade and return home safely, but Cão was the first of the more professional explorers.

Portuguese compass
One of the few instruments that Portuguese sailors had to help them find their way was a magnetic compass – a simpler version of this 18th-century model. It contained a magnetized iron needle. If allowed to swing freely, the needle pointed roughly north and south to show in which direction a ship was sailing.

BARTOLEMEU DIAS
Dias was sent out to continue the work of Diogo Cão and find a sea route to India. Throughout the voyage he set up *padrões*, such as this one, along the coast. He sailed farther south than Cão, becoming the first Portuguese explorer to sail round Africa and enter the Indian Ocean in 1488. Dias wanted to sail on and try to reach India, but his scared and weary crew forced him to turn back.

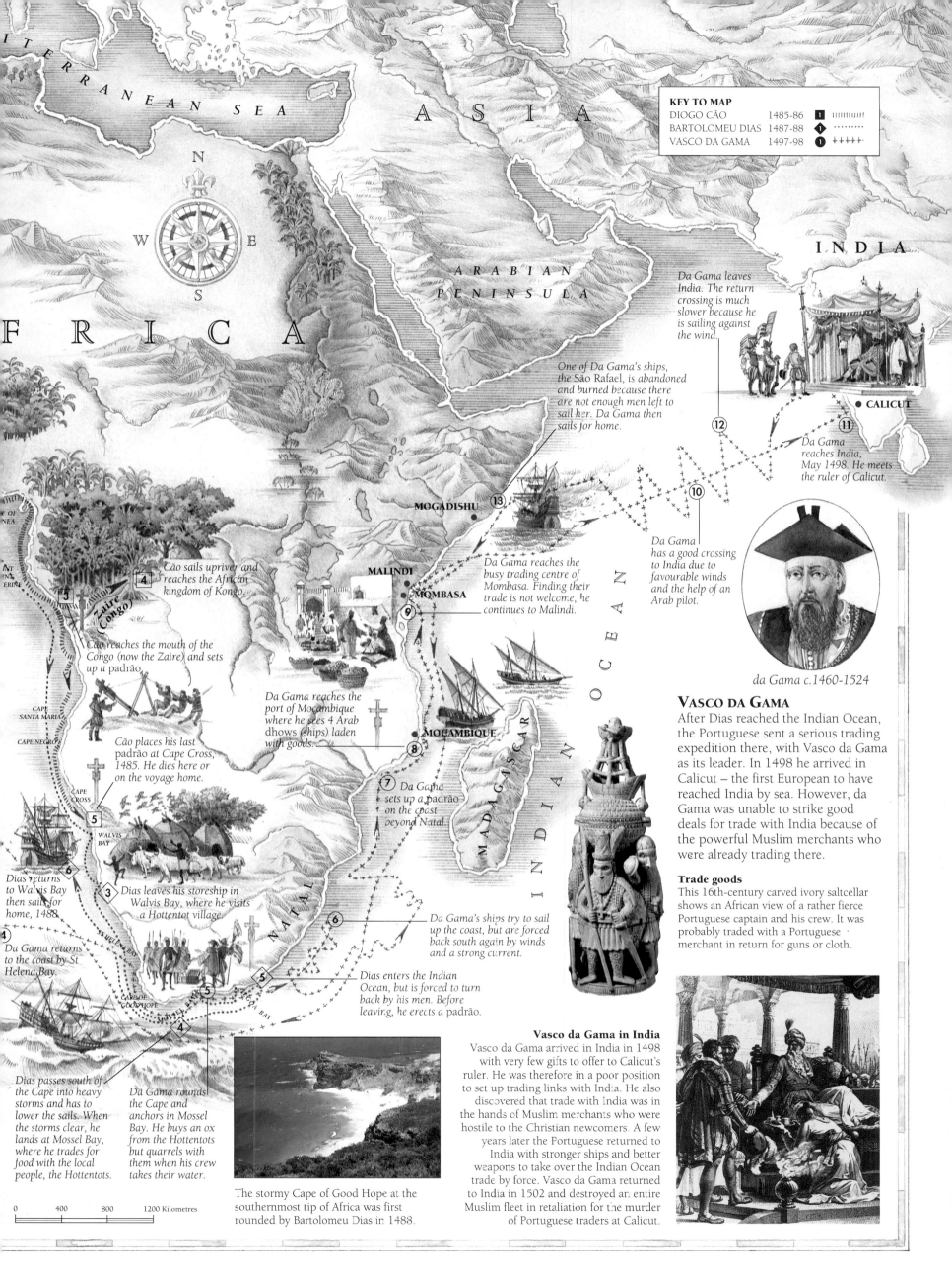

MEDITERRANEAN SEA

ASIA

AFRICA

N E W S

ARABIAN PENINSULA

INDIA

Da Gama leaves India. The return crossing is much slower because he is sailing against the wind.

One of Da Gama's ships, the São Rafael, is abandoned and burned because there are not enough men left to sail her. Da Gama then sails for home.

Da Gama reaches India, May 1498. He meets the ruler of Calicut.

● CALICUT

⑫

⑪

⑬

MOGADISHU

Da Gama has a good crossing to India due to favourable winds and the help of an Arab pilot.

⑩

Da Gama reaches the busy trading centre of Mombasa. Finding their trade is not welcome, he continues to Malindi.

MALINDI

MOMBASA

⑨

Cão sails upriver and reaches the African kingdom of Kongo.

④

Zaire (Congo)

Cão reaches the mouth of the Congo (now the Zaire) and sets up a padrão.

③

da Gama c.1460-1524

VASCO DA GAMA

After Dias reached the Indian Ocean, the Portuguese sent a serious trading expedition there, with Vasco da Gama as its leader. In 1498 he arrived in Calicut – the first European to have reached India by sea. However, da Gama was unable to strike good deals for trade with India because of the powerful Muslim merchants who were already trading there.

CAPE SANTA MARIA

CAPE NEGRO

Cão places his last padrão at Cape Cross, 1485. He dies here or on the voyage home.

CAPE CROSS

⑤

WALVIS BAY

Da Gama reaches the port of Moçambique where he sees 4 Arab dhows (ships) laden with goods.

⑧

● MOÇAMBIQUE

MADAGASCAR

⑦ Da Gama sets up a padrão on the coast beyond Natal.

Trade goods
This 16th-century carved ivory saltcellar shows an African view of a rather fierce Portuguese captain and his crew. It was probably traded with a Portuguese merchant in return for guns or cloth.

Dias returns to Walvis Bay then sails for home, 1488.

⑥

Dias leaves his storeship in Walvis Bay, where he visits a Hottentot village.

③

Da Gama returns to the coast by St Helena Bay.

④

NATAL

INDIAN OCEAN

⑥ Da Gama's ships try to sail up the coast, but are forced back south again by winds and a strong current.

Dias enters the Indian Ocean, but is forced to turn back by his men. Before leaving, he erects a padrão.

⑤

CAPE OF GOOD HOPE

MOSSEL BAY

⑤

④

Dias passes south of the Cape into heavy storms and has to lower the sails. When the storms clear, he lands at Mossel Bay, where he trades for food with the local people, the Hottentots.

Da Gama rounds the Cape and anchors in Mossel Bay. He buys an ox from the Hottentots but quarrels with them when his crew takes their water.

0   400   800   1200 Kilometres

The stormy Cape of Good Hope at the southernmost tip of Africa was first rounded by Bartolomeu Dias in 1488.

Vasco da Gama in India
Vasco da Gama arrived in India in 1498 with very few gifts to offer to Calicut's ruler. He was therefore in a poor position to set up trading links with India. He also discovered that trade with India was in the hands of Muslim merchants who were hostile to the Christian newcomers. A few years later the Portuguese returned to India with stronger ships and better weapons to take over the Indian Ocean trade by force. Vasco da Gama returned to India in 1502 and destroyed an entire Muslim fleet in retaliation for the murder of Portuguese traders at Calicut.

COLUMBUS AND THE NEW WORLD

WHILE THE PORTUGUESE were trying to find a sea route to Asia by sailing around Africa, a Genoese sailor named Christopher Columbus thought of a different way of getting there. He decided to sail west, convinced that, as the world is round, sooner or later he must reach Asia from the opposite direction. He set out in 1492, having persuaded the Spanish king and queen to pay for his voyage.

In those days, people thought that the globe was much smaller than it really is. They imagined that one huge piece of land – made up of Europe, Asia, and Africa – stretched most of the way around the world, and had no idea that the Americas existed. As a result, Columbus made one of the biggest mistakes, yet greatest discoveries, in the history of exploration. He came to some islands roughly where he expected to find Asia and thought that he was approaching the East Indies near mainland Asia. He made four voyages across the Atlantic without realizing that instead of finding Asia, he had found a "New World."

Columbus 1451-1506

CHRISTOPHER COLUMBUS

Columbus was born in the North Italian port of Genoa, which was famous for its skilled sailors. He was named after St Christopher, the patron saint of travellers. As a young man, he went to work in Lisbon, Portugal, the centre of European navigation and ocean voyaging in the 15th century. While he was making charts for the Portuguese, he began forming his great plan of sailing west to Asia.

Prayers in a strange land

Religion was an important part of life on board a 15th-century Spanish ship. Columbus believed that God was guiding him and everyone on board his ships attended prayers twice a day. The Spanish thought that it was their duty to convert the native people to Christianity, and that if you were not a Christian, you were not fully a human being. Here, the crew celebrate Mass on the Isle of Pines, while curious local people observe this unfamiliar custom.

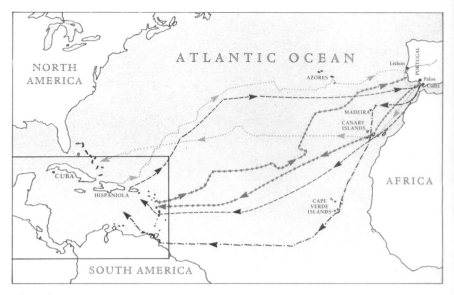

The Atlantic voyages (1492-1504)

This map shows the routes Columbus took across the Atlantic. On his first voyage he reached Watling Island, Cuba and Hispaniola; on the second, he built settlements on Hispaniola and explored Jamaica; and on the third he reached Trinidad. His fourth voyage in 1502 was a last desperate attempt to find Asia. He landed in Central America, but did not realize the value of his discovery and returned to Spain in 1504.

KEY TO MAPS
CHRISTOPHER COLUMBUS
1st voyage	1492-93	❶ ··········
2nd voyage	1493-96	❺ +++++++
3rd voyage	1498-1500	❿ –o–o–o–
4th voyage	1502-04	❻ – – – – –

Columbus leaves Jamaica and sails west along the coast of Cuba where he sees turtles and his first flamingoes. He turns back, without realizing that Cuba is an island, not part of mainland Asia.

Columbus reaches the Bay Islands off the coast of Central America and sails east into stormy seas.

Columbus sails round a cape into calmer waters. He names the cape Gracias a Dios – "Thanks to God".

Columbus's ships anchor off the Rio Grande and 2 of his men drown going ashore to fetch wood and water.

Columbus is forced to leave Belén by hostile locals.

New World discoveries

When he reached the West Indies, Columbus was disappointed not to find the rich Asian trading cities he expected. However, he did make many discoveries. He and his crew tasted foods that were new to them, such as pineapples, potatoes, and sweetcorn, which they called "Indian corn". They were fascinated by the strange habits of the Arawak people of Cuba, who rolled the dried leaves of a plant (tobacco) into a tube, set light to it, and puffed smoke.

Columbus's ships

On his first voyage, Columbus took three ships. The largest of these was the *Santa Maria*. She had three masts and was square-rigged (square sails on the main- and foremasts). The huge sail on the mainmast provided most of the driving power. With a crew of 40, space on board was very limited. Food had to be cooked on the open deck. Columbus had a small cabin with a bunk; his crew slept in roll-up beds on deck or among the cargo. The other two ships, the *Pinta* and *Nina* (Columbus's favourite), were much smaller.

0   100   200   300 Kilometres

Columbus and his crew first sight land, Oct 1492. They land on an island, which he names San Salvador.

1

WATLING ISLAND
(SAN SALVADOR)

RUM CAY

LONG ISLAND

CROOKED ISLAND

Columbus reaches Cuba and is disappointed to find no trace of Asia.

2

The Santa Maria is wrecked off the coast of Hispaniola. Columbus claims the island for Spain and builds the fort of Navidad.

3

Columbus finds Arawaks have killed many of his men at Navidad. He builds a new settlement – Isabela.

6

"ISABELA"

"NAVIDAD"

Columbus in chains

Columbus was a magnificent sailor but a poor governor – he found new lands, but he did not look after his settlements well. He was proud and sometimes boastful, which made him several enemies among the Spaniards who followed him to the New World. When he returned to Hispaniola on his third voyage, the Spanish king and queen received complaints about him. They sent a new governor to the island who arrested Columbus, bound him in chains, and sent him back to Spain. He remained in chains for several weeks until a royal order came for his release.

Columbus leaves 40 of his men at Navidad and sets sail for Spain, Jan 1493.

4

Columbus arrives in Dominica with 17 ships, Nov 1493. He sails to Guadeloupe where some of his men get lost in the forest. The islanders, Caribs, are said to be cannibals, but no one is eaten!

PUERTO RICO

MONA

ST CROIX

ATLANTIC OCEAN

SANTO DOMINGO

HISPANIOLA

12

8

ANTIGUA

Columbus sets sail for Spain, 1496.

GUADELOUPE

9

5

DOMINICA

JAMAICA

20

WEST INDIES

14

Columbus sails south of Jamaica. A strong current carries him west towards Cuba. From here he sails due south in search of Asia.

Columbus leaves Jamaica. His ships are too leaky and worm-eaten to repair, so he sails for Spain in a new ship, 1503.

Columbus anchors at Santo Domingo. The new governor arrests him and sends him back to Spain.

Columbus sails to the island of Mona, then visits his settlement at Isabela.

Columbus lands in Martinique at the start of his 4th voyage, June 1502. He sails for Hispaniola.

13

MARTINIQUE

CARIBBEAN SEA

BEATA

ST LUCIA

BARBADOS

WINDWARD ISLANDS

The lush green vegetation of St Lucia, one of the islands in the Windward group. Columbus was amazed by the beauty of these islands, but disappointed to find no trace of Asia.

Columbus sees men diving down to oyster beds in search of pearls. He plans to buy some on his way back, but he never returns.

11

Columbus sets a more southerly course via Trinidad for his 3rd voyage, July 1498.

ISLA MARGARITA

GOLFO DE PARIA

TRINIDAD

10

Columbus sails along the coast to Mosquito Point where he and his crew see their first alligator. Further west, he stops to build the settlement of Belén.

18

MOSQUITO POINT

N
W   E
S

Orinoco

SOUTH AMERICA

THE NORTH-WEST PASSAGE

THE MAIN REASON for European voyages of discovery in the 15th century was to search for a sea trade route to the Far East. The Portuguese found a route by sailing east around Africa; the Spaniards found a western route around South America. However, both routes were long and difficult. The English and the Dutch tried to find alternatives. There were two possibilities: north-east over the top of Siberia, or north-west over the top of North America. These routes were known as the North-East and North-West Passages. The English took the lead in searching for the North-West Passage. For more than 300 years they explored the coast of what are now the United States and Canada. In the 19th century, Sir John Franklin's expedition almost found it. When his ships went missing, those that went in search of him did find the passage, though no one sailed through it until the Norwegian explorer, Roald Amundsen, in 1906. The North-West Passage never became popular as a shipping route because it is blocked with ice all year.

JOHN CABOT

Cabot was an Italian navigator who, like Columbus, believed he could reach the East by sailing west. In 1497 he set out on a voyage in the *Matthew*. The merchants of Bristol, England, paid for most of his voyage. He reached Newfoundland in Canada and, thinking it was Asia, returned to England in triumph. In 1498 he set out again, but the voyage ended in disaster. Cabot was never seen again.

MARTIN FROBISHER

Frobisher was a tough English adventurer. As a young man he went on trading voyages to Africa. In 1576 he sailed in search of a North-West Passage. Near the Canadian coast, he found the inlet now called Frobisher Bay. His search ended there when his men found a glittering rock, which they thought was gold. They loaded their ship with it and sailed for home – only to find that it was "fool's gold".

Frobisher c.1535-1594

Amundsen completes the voyage through the North-West Passage, sailing through the Bering Strait, and reaching Nome, Aug 1906.

Beechey Island in the Canadian Arctic, where the Franklin expedition spent the winter of 1845-46.

Franklin sails west of King William Island. His ships become trapped in ice, Sept 1846. All their men die.

Franklin's expedition set up camp on Beechey Island, 1845.

Hudson died 1611

HENRY HUDSON

Hudson, an Englishman, was one of the most experienced navigators of his day. He sailed several times in search of the North-East, as well as the North-West, Passage, working for the Dutch or the English. For the Dutch, he discovered the Hudson River, where Dutch settlers founded the port that became New York City. In 1610 he set out, for the English, on his last voyage to look for the North-West Passage, but he never returned.

BERING SEA

NOME

ARCTIC CIRCLE

MELVILLE ISLAND

BANKS ISLAND

VICTORIA ISLAND

Franklin's ships abandoned here

KING WILLIAM ISLAND

GJOA HAVEN

Amundsen's men spend a 3rd winter in the Arctic. All but one survive with help from the Inuit and some American whalers in the area.

Mackenzie

PACIFIC OCEAN

Amundsen's expedition spends 2 winters at Gjoa Haven. They learn how to handle dog sledges and to live like the Inuit.

Mutiny in Hudson Bay

In August 1610, Hudson discovered a narrow passage of water in Canada. It led him, not to the Pacific, as he thought, but into the huge inland sea that is now named after him – Hudson Bay. His ship, the *Discovery*, sailed all the way down the east coast of the bay, where it was trapped by ice. Hudson and his crew spent a miserable winter there. In the summer, the ice melted and the ship was freed, but the crew, who believed Hudson had been keeping a secret store of food, mutinied. They forced him, his young son, and seven loyal sailors into a small boat with no oars and left them to die.

N W E S

N C A M

Franklin 1786-1847

JOHN FRANKLIN

Sir John Franklin volunteered to lead an important expedition to complete the discovery of the North-West Passage in 1845. He had spent the last seven years as Governor of Tasmania and was past retirement age, but his experience as an explorer and naval officer persuaded the British Admiralty that he was the best person for the job. He set off in May 1845 and was never seen again.

A last message

This note provided vital clues about the last sad days of the Franklin expedition. It was found in a tin cylinder buried on King William Island in 1859. The note, signed by two of Franklin's officers, records Franklin's death in 1847. It also reports that, after the expedition's two ships had been stuck in the ice for a year and a half, the crews tried to reach safety by travelling south overland. Not one man survived.

The search for Franklin

After the disappearance of the Franklin expedition in 1846, a huge international effort was made to find him and his men. By 1850 there were 14 ships in the Arctic looking for him. Lady Franklin sent several expeditions to search for her husband. Francis McClintock led one such expedition in the *Fox* (a small steam yacht that belonged to Lady Franklin). In 1859 a party of his men solved the mystery. On King William Island, they found a tin cylinder buried in a mound of stones. Inside was the document (shown left) that explained what had happened.

Finding clues

This medicine chest comes from one of Franklin's ships. McClintock's expedition found it on King William Island. Inside were cotton wool and jars of old medicines, including a tin of ginger (used for stomach upsets).

0   200   400   600 Kilometres

Frobisher sails via southern Iceland and sights Greenland, which he mistakes for a new land, June 1576.

GREENLAND

ICELAND

Amundsen and his crew pick up stores left by whaling ships. Inuit help them load the ship.

Hudson leaves London and sails west in the Discovery, 1610. He approaches the south coast of Greenland.

Franklin, commanding the Erebus and Terror, enters Davis Strait, June 1845.

Amundsen sails from Norway in the Gjöa, 1903. He has wisely chosen a very small ship with a crew of only 6.

GODHAVN

Amundsen stops at Godhavn in Greenland and trades with the Inuit.

BAFFIN ISLAND

DAVIS STRAIT

Frobisher and his men find rocks which they think are gold. They load their ship and sail for home.

FROBISHER BAY

Frobisher meets several Inuit and thinks they are Chinese. He captures one man and takes him back to England where he dies of a cold.

HUDSON STRAIT

Hudson enters the "great and whirling sea" of Hudson Bay.

HUDSON BAY

ATLANTIC OCEAN

Cabot sights Newfoundland, 24 June 1497. He discovers the fishery of the Grand Banks, where there are so many codfish that you can scoop them up in a basket.

NEWFOUNDLAND

The Discovery is frozen in for the winter. The following June, the crew mutiny and Hudson is marooned in the bay.

NORTH

AMERICA

Cabot runs short of supplies and has to turn back.

Franklin's ship Erebus (32 m long)

Amundsen's ship Gjöa (21 m long)

Through the North-West Passage

The first voyage through the whole North-West Passage, from the Atlantic to the Pacific, was made in the *Gjöa*. She was a Norwegian fishing boat, about one-eighth the size of Franklin's *Erebus*. In command was the Norwegian explorer Roald Amundsen, who later became the first person to reach the South Pole. The *Gjöa* left Norway in 1903 with enough provisions for five years. During the course of the expedition, Amundsen spent three winters in the Arctic, learning how the Inuit (Eskimos) lived and travelled.

KEY TO MAP

JOHN CABOT	1497	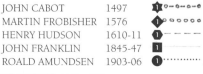
MARTIN FROBISHER	1576	
HENRY HUDSON	1610-11	
JOHN FRANKLIN	1845-47	
ROALD AMUNDSEN	1903-06	

THE NORTH-EAST PASSAGE

WHILE THE ENGLISH concentrated their efforts on searching for a North-West Passage from Europe to the Far East, the Dutch tried to find a North-East Passage. In the 16th century the Dutch started to sail east along the north Siberian coast and began to trade with Muscovy (Russia). They built a base for their merchants near Kola. From there Dutch ships slowly edged their way farther east, reaching Novaya Zemlya in 1584. Willem Barents' expedition of 1596 made the greatest progress, but the Dutch eventually abandoned the search, defeated by the treacherous icy seas.

No one knew for sure if the North-East Passage really existed until Russian explorer, Semyon Dezhnev explored the Arctic coast of Siberia in the 17th century. Even then, it did not seem a possible route for large ships. It was a Finnish explorer, Nils Nordenskjöld, who finally completed the passage nearly 300 years later in 1879, in a tough whaling ship. Today, Russian icebreakers keep the channel free of ice for shipping.

Barents 1550-1597

WILLEM BARENTS

Barents was born on an island off the Dutch coast and knew the sea well. He was a first-rate navigator, and in 1594 was chosen by Captain Jakob Van Heemskerck to be the pilot for an expedition in search of the North-East Passage. The weather was unusually mild and he got as far as the Kara Sea. His next two voyages were less successful – temperatures were bitterly cold and progress through the thick sea-ice was difficult and dangerous.

Overwintering in the Arctic
On his third voyage in 1596, Barents was entering the Kara Sea when the ice closed in behind his ship. The Dutch were trapped for the winter. They built the hut shown here from driftwood. Inside, there was a huge fireplace and a kind of turkish bath, made from barrels. Despite these comforts, it was so cold that icicles formed on the bunks. They lived on the ship's stores and by hunting animals, and became the first Europeans to survive a winter in the Arctic.

Whaling log
Whalers and sealers were the first Europeans to make a living in Arctic waters. They sometimes made new discoveries about the region, which they recorded in their logs (ship's journals). These pages from a 19th-century whaler's log give details about the day's sailing and the day's catch. They include drawings and measurements of the flukes (tails) of two whales.

KEY TO MAP
WILLEM BARENTS	1596-98	**1** ++++++
SEMYON DEZHNEV	1648	**1** ○○○○○○
NILS NORDENSKJÖLD	1878-79	**1** –○–○–○–

0   200   400   600   800 Kilometres

Barents discovers Bear Island – so named because of a long fight with a polar bear.

Barents sails further north and discovers Spitsbergen. Here, the Dutch see their first reindeer.

Barents sails north of Novaya Zemlya, where his ship gets stuck in ice. He and his crew build a hut on shore for the winter, Sept 1596.

ARCTIC

SPITSBERGEN

FRANZ JOSEF LAND

BEAR ISLAND

BRITISH ISLES

ATLANTIC OCEAN

NORTH SEA

BARENTS SEA

NOVAYA ZEMLYA

KARA SEA

2 TROMSO

Nordenskjold boards the Vega at Tromso and the expedition begins, July 1878.

GOTHENBURG

1 AMSTERDAM
Barents sets out with a Dutch expedition, May 1596.

KOLA

Barents's crew reach Kola, July 1597. Barents dies on the way there.

5

1 KARLSKRONA

The Vega leaves Karlskrona, June 1878.

EUROPE

3 KHABAROVO

Nordenskjold stops at Khabarovo, where the Samoyed people live in turf-covered cabins with their reindeer.

4

MEDITERRANEAN SEA

Nordenskjold reaches the Mediterranean and sails for home.

9

BLACK SEA

Ob

ASIA

NILS NORDENSKJÖLD

Nordenskjöld, a Finn who settled in Sweden, trained as a geologist and chemist before becoming one of the greatest scientific explorers. He made several early expeditions to the Arctic, which prepared him well for the harsh climate, thick fogs, and dangerous icy channels he would encounter while sailing through the North-East Passage. He left Norway on board the *Vega* in July 1878 and a year later, reached the Pacific Ocean, becoming the first explorer to sail through the North-East Passage.

Nordenskjöld 1832-1901

At Cape Chelyuskin

The voyage of the *Vega* was an important scientific expedition, as well as an attempt to sail through the North-East Passage. Throughout the voyage, the crew made scientific observations about the region. When they reached Cape Chelyuskin, the most northern point of mainland Asia, some of the crew set up the monument shown right; others used special instruments to measure the shape of the land. The information they brought back was later used to make a map of the region.

In 1596, Willem Barents became the first European to sail through the dangerous icy waters to the islands of Spitsbergen.

The Vega

Nordenskjöld's ship, the *Vega*, was a 300-tonne whaling ship, built in Germany in 1872. The hull was made of oak, with an outer skin of tougher wood to resist the sharp pressure of the ice. Besides sails, the *Vega* had a powerful steam engine. After her famous voyage through the North-East Passage, the *Vega* returned to duty as a whaling ship.

Chukchi

The Chukchi are a group of people who live in north-eastern Siberia. Traditionally, they live in huts dug into the ground and survive by hunting and fishing, although some groups herd reindeer and move from place to place. Nordenskjöld's expedition first saw the Chukchi at Cape Shelagskiy. At that time they had had very little contact with strangers, but they were very friendly to Nordenskjöld and his crew and helped them on their way.

Semyon Dezhnev

The north-eastern point of Asia is called Cape Dezhnev, after the Russian explorer Semyon Dezhnev. In 1648, he is said to have sailed east from the River Kolyma on the Arctic coast, round the cape, through the Bering Strait, and down to the River Anadyr on the Pacific coast. He used a small, flat-bottomed boat, called a *koch*. Unfortunately, the full details of this voyage are not known, because Dezhnev's records were lost.

Today the North-East Passage is no longer dangerous, thanks to ships called ice-breakers that clear the way. It has become a busy commercial waterway with large ships passing through it daily.

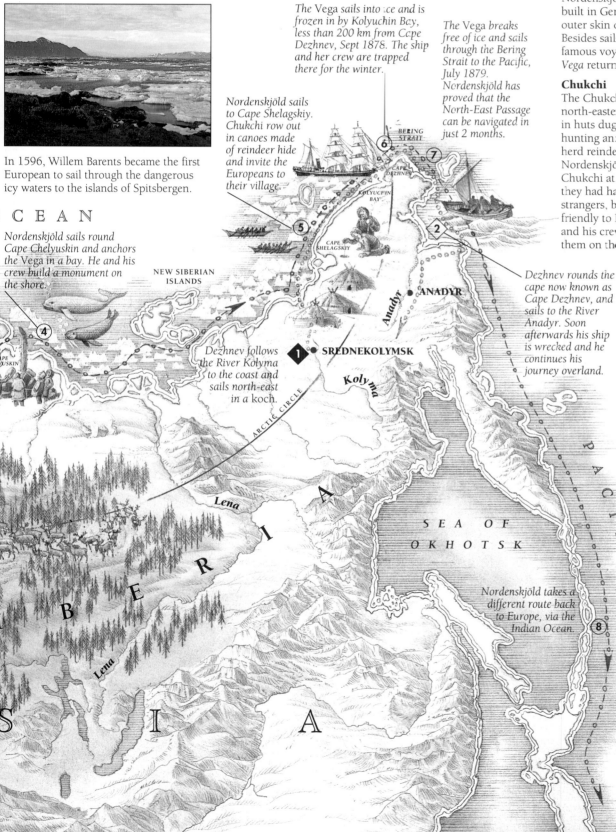

The Vega sails into ice and is frozen in by Kolyuchin Bay, less than 200 km from Cape Dezhnev, Sept 1878. The ship and her crew are trapped there for the winter.

The Vega breaks free of ice and sails through the Bering Strait to the Pacific, July 1879. Nordenskjöld has proved that the North-East Passage can be navigated in just 2 months.

Nordenskjöld sails to Cape Shelagskiy. Chukchi row out in canoes made of reindeer hide and invite the Europeans to their village.

Nordenskjöld sails round Cape Chelyuskin and anchors the Vega in a bay. He and his crew build a monument on the shore.

NEW SIBERIAN ISLANDS

CAPE CHELYUSKIN

BERING STRAIT

CAPE DEZHNEV

KOLYUCHIN BAY

CAPE SHELAGSKIY

Anadyr • ANADYR

Dezhnev rounds the cape now known as Cape Dezhnev, and sails to the River Anadyr. Soon afterwards his ship is wrecked and he continues his journey overland.

■ SREDNEKOLYMSK

Dezhnev follows the River Kolyma to the coast and sails north-east in a koch.

Kolyma

ARCTIC CIRCLE

OCEAN

SIBERIA

Lena

Lena

SEA OF OKHOTSK

Nordenskjöld takes a different route back to Europe, via the Indian Ocean.

PACIFIC OCEAN

ACROSS SIBERIA

AT THE START OF the 18th century, Peter the Great, Tsar of Russia, was determined to make his weak and backward country a great, modern empire. At that time, Siberia – the vast expanse of land to the east of his empire – was still mostly unexplored. He decided to bring it under Russian control. This would give Russia some useful ports on the Pacific Ocean. He also hoped to discover whether or not Asia was really joined to North America, as he believed.

In 1724, the Tsar appointed Vitus Bering to lead the first expedition. His orders were to go to Kamchatka, in eastern Siberia, and build boats there. Then he was to sail north to find out whether North America and Asia were joined. The orders were simple, but the task was not. Bering returned without having proved for certain that Asia and North America are separated by sea. In 1734 Bering was placed in charge of an ambitious new project, known as the Great Northern Expedition. Its aim was to reach Alaska and what is now called the Bering Sea, and to explore the entire Arctic coast of Siberia.

Bering 1681-1741

VITUS BERING

Bering, a Dane, went to sea as a young man. He met a Norwegian who was an admiral in the Russian navy (Peter the Great employed many foreigners) and decided to join the Russian navy himself. On his return to St Petersburg in 1730, after the Kamchatka expedition, he was told he had not done enough. He had not proved that Asia and America were one land mass. In 1734 he set off again, this time to join the Great Northern Expedition.

The Great Northern Expedition

This expedition was organized by the Imperial Admiralty College in St Petersburg, with the advice of Bering and others. Bering himself travelled across Russia to the Pacific, and the job of exploring the northern coast was given to a group of young Russian officers. The coast was divided into five sections: from Archangel to the River Ob (explored by Muravyov and Pavlov, then Malgin); from the Ob to the Yenisei (explored by Ovtzin); from the Yenisei to the tip of the Taimyr peninsula (Minim, then K. Laptev); from the River Lena westward to the Taimyr peninsula (explored by Prochinchev, then Chelyuskin); and from the Lena around East Cape to the River Anadyr (assigned to Dimitri Laptev). It took nearly 10 years to complete this series of expeditions.

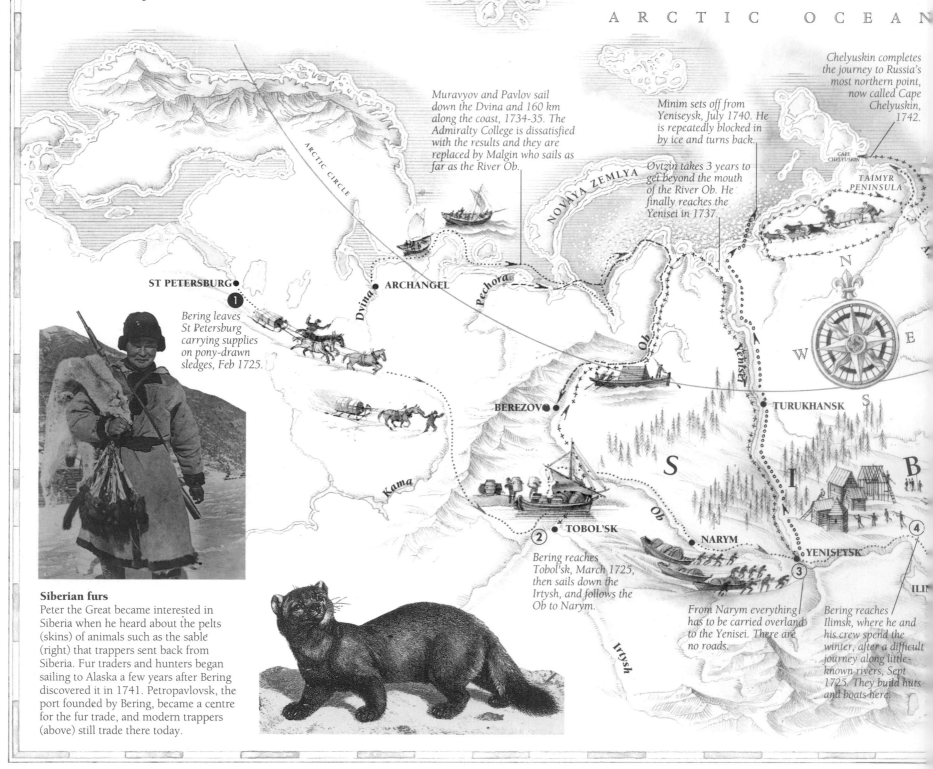

ARCTIC OCEAN

Muravyov and Pavlov sail down the Dvina and 160 km along the coast, 1734-35. The Admiralty College is dissatisfied with the results and they are replaced by Malgin who sails as far as the River Ob.

Minim sets off from Yeniseysk, July 1740. He is repeatedly blocked in by ice and turns back.

Chelyuskin completes the journey to Russia's most northern point, now called Cape Chelyuskin, 1742.

Ovtzin takes 3 years to get beyond the mouth of the River Ob. He finally reaches the Yenisei in 1737.

ARCTIC CIRCLE

NOVAYA ZEMLYA

CAPE CHELYUSKIN

TAIMYR PENINSULA

ST PETERSBURG

1 *Bering leaves St Petersburg carrying supplies on pony-drawn sledges, Feb 1725.*

ARCHANGEL

Dvina

Pechora

Ob

Yenisei

TURUKHANSK

BEREZOV

Kama

S I B

2 TOBOL'SK

Bering reaches Tobol'sk, March 1725, then sails down the Irtysh, and follows the Ob to Narym.

Ob

NARYM

YENISEYSK

3

4

ILI

From Narym everything has to be carried overland to the Yenisei. There are no roads.

Bering reaches Ilimsk, where he and his crew spend the winter, after a difficult journey along little-known rivers, Sept 1725. They build huts and boats here.

Irtysh

Siberian furs

Peter the Great became interested in Siberia when he heard about the pelts (skins) of animals such as the sable (right) that trappers sent back from Siberia. Fur traders and hunters began sailing to Alaska a few years after Bering discovered it in 1741. Petropavlovsk, the port founded by Bering, became a centre for the fur trade, and modern trappers (above) still trade there today.

Down the Arctic rivers
The explorers on the Great Northern Expedition had to travel great distances down ice-choked rivers through parts of Siberia that are much colder than the North Pole. The Russian Admiralty College provided plenty of men for the Great Northern Expedition, but not enough back-up support. Their only supplies were what they could carry with them in small boats (above) and on sledges. Often, nothing was heard of the explorers until they returned years later.

Prochinchev tries to reach the Taimyr peninsula, via the River Lena. He almost succeeds, but dies. He is buried near the River Olenek.

D. Laptev sails down the River Lena and, after 5 years, reaches the Kolyma. With dog teams, he completes the trek overland to the Anadyr, 1741.

A L A S K A

ST ELIAS MOUNTAINS

KODIAK ISLAND

Bering sights the snowy mountains of Alaska, July 1741. Sick and short of food, he does not stay long.
⑫

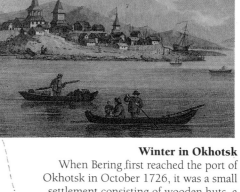

Bering anchors off Kodiak Island. He allows the ship's naturalist less than one day to collect plant specimens.
⑬

Winter in Okhotsk
When Bering first reached the port of Okhotsk in October 1726, it was a small settlement consisting of wooden huts, a small fort, and a couple of churches. He spent the winter there, while his carpenters built a boat to carry his expedition party across the Sea of Okhotsk to Kamchatka. It would have been simpler to sail round the tip of the peninsula but the route was unknown and Bering thought the voyage would be too risky.

Bering sails through the Bering Strait, Aug 1728. Fog prevents him seeing land. Chirikov wants to go on, but Bering is satisfied.
⑨

BERING STRAIT
EAST CAPE

B E R I N G   S E A

A L E U T I A N   I S L A N D S

Bering sets off north in the Gabriel, with 44 men, July 1728. A group of local people, the Chukchi, row out to the ship.
⑧

After a stormy voyage, Bering and his men land on an island (now called Bering Island), Nov 1741. Bering dies. His men survive by eating sea creatures.

BERING ISLAND
⑭

Bering's ships
On his second expedition, Bering built the St Peter (above) and the St Paul. The St Paul was commanded by a Russian captain, Alexei Chirikov. Both ships reached Alaska, but only the St Paul returned safely.

Anadyr

Kolyma

ARCTIC CIRCLE

Yana

Lena

Bering's ships set sail from Petropavlovsk, June 1741.
⑪

PETROPAVLOVSK

KAMCHATKA

BOLSHERETSK

OKHOTSK

⑦

Bering's expedition crosses the Sea of Okhotsk and Kamchatka where the Gabriel is built.

⑥

S I B E R I A

YAKUTSK

⑤

Bering's men eat ponies which have died of cold on the journey from Yakutsk. They build huts at Okhotsk for the winter.

SEA OF OKHOTSK

⑩

The Gabriel returns to Kamchatka for the winter. Bering himself continues on to St Petersburg.

Bering divides the expedition into 3 parties at Yakutsk, the last town before the coast, June 1726.

Lena

0 100 200 300 400 500 Kilometres

KEY TO MAP
VITUS BERING
1st expedition	1725-29	❶ · · · · · · ·
2nd expedition	1734-41	⓫ — — —

GREAT NORTHERN EXPEDITION
Muravyov & Pavlov	1734-35	· · · · · · ·
Malgin	1735-37	— — — —
Ovtzin	1734-37	+ + + + +
Minim & K. Laptev	1739-41	ooooooo
Prochinchev	1735	÷ + + + +
Chelyuskin	1742	÷ + + + +
D. Laptev	1735-41	— - - - —

The death of Bering
Exhausted and ill, Bering died on Bering Island in 1741, on the return voyage from Alaska. His men were suffering from scurvy and had to spend the winter on the island. In the spring they built a boat from the remains of the St Peter, and sailed back to Petropavlovsk, 482 km away. Chirikov, who was in the St Paul, had sailed farther along the Alaskan coast than Bering and got most of his men back safely to Petropavlovsk. He never recovered from the hardships of the voyage, however, and died three years later.

AROUND THE WORLD

WHEN THE SHIPS of Spain and Portugal dominated the world's oceans, the greatest voyage of all was led by a Portuguese, Ferdinand Magellan, in the Spanish ship *Victoria* in 1519. It was the first expedition to sail around the world, although this had not been Magellan's original intention. He was trying to find a route to the Spice Islands (now the Moluccas) and thought that they – and the continent of Asia – were not far from America. He hoped to find a sea passage through America that would lead him to his destination. The Portuguese had already found a route to the East, around Africa and India, but that route was forbidden to Spain by the Treaty of Tordesillas. Magellan set out to prove it was possible to reach the Spice Islands by a western route. More than 60 years later British explorer, Francis Drake, led the next expedition to sail around the world.

The Treaty of Tordesillas

To prevent quarrels, Pope Alexander VI suggested dividing up the undiscovered world between Spain and Portugal – the two leading European powers at that time. Under the Treaty of Tordesillas (1494) a line was drawn through the Atlantic on this map. The two powers negotiated where the line would fall. West of that line, unexplored lands were claimed by Spain. East of the line, they were claimed by Portugal. When the coast of Brazil was explored it turned out to be in the Portuguese half. So where was the boundary between Spain and Portugal on the far side of the world? Were the Spice Islands (the Moluccas) in Portuguese territory, or in the Spanish half, as Magellan believed?

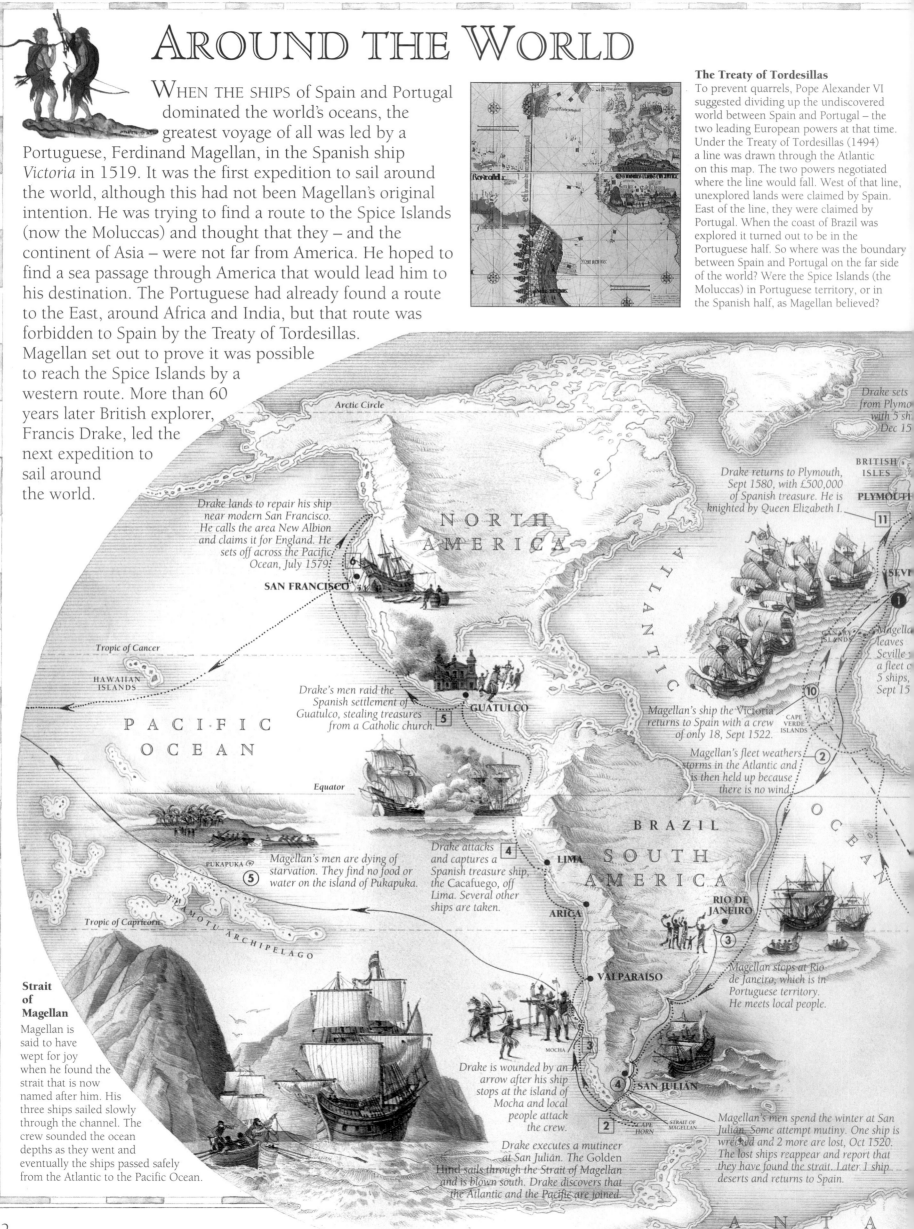

Arctic Circle

NORTH AMERICA

Drake lands to repair his ship near modern San Francisco. He calls the area New Albion and claims it for England. He sets off across the Pacific Ocean, July 1579.

SAN FRANCISCO 6

Tropic of Cancer

HAWAIIAN ISLANDS

Drake's men raid the Spanish settlement of Guatulco, stealing treasures from a Catholic church.

GUATULCO 5

PACIFIC OCEAN

Equator

PUKAPUKA

Magellan's men are dying of starvation. They find no food or water on the island of Pukapuka. 5

Tropic of Capricorn

TUAMOTU ARCHIPELAGO

Strait of Magellan

Magellan is said to have wept for joy when he found the strait that is now named after him. His three ships sailed slowly through the channel. The crew sounded the ocean depths as they went and eventually the ships passed safely from the Atlantic to the Pacific Ocean.

Drake is wounded by an arrow after his ship stops at the island of Mocha and local people attack the crew.

MOCHA 3

Drake executes a mutineer at San Julián. The Golden Hind sails through the Strait of Magellan and is blown south. Drake discovers that the Atlantic and the Pacific are joined.

Drake attacks and captures a Spanish treasure ship, the Cacafuego, off Lima. Several other ships are taken. 4

LIMA

ARICA

BRAZIL
SOUTH AMERICA

VALPARAÍSO

RIO DE JANEIRO 3

Magellan stops at Rio de Janeiro, which is in Portuguese territory. He meets local people.

SAN JULIÁN 4

CAPE HORN 2

STRAIT OF MAGELLAN

Magellan's men spend the winter at San Julián. Some attempt mutiny. One ship is wrecked and 2 more are lost, Oct 1520. The lost ships reappear and report that they have found the strait. Later 1 ship deserts and returns to Spain.

ATLANTIC OCEAN

Drake returns to Plymouth, Sept 1580, with £500,000 of Spanish treasure. He is knighted by Queen Elizabeth I.

BRITISH ISLES

PLYMOUTH 11

SEV[ILLE] 1

Magellan leaves Seville [with] a fleet [of] 5 ships, Sept 15[19]

Drake sets [off] from Plymo[uth] with 5 sh[ips] Dec 15[77]

Magellan's ship the Victoria returns to Spain with a crew of only 18, Sept 1522.

CAPE VERDE ISLANDS 10

Magellan's fleet weathers storms in the Atlantic and is then held up because there is no wind. 2

CANARY ISLANDS

ANTA[RCTICA]

FERDINAND MAGELLAN

Magellan was a Portuguese knight and adventurer who had taken part in Portuguese expeditions to India. He quarrelled with the king of Portugal, left the country in 1514 and entered the service of the king of Spain. In 1519 he presented the king of Spain with his plan for reaching the Spice Islands (Moluccas) by sailing west. Impressed by the possibility of great riches for Spain, the king gave Magellan the command of a Spanish expedition to look for a strait through America to Asia. It consisted of five ships and about 260 men. Only one ship and 18 men saw Spain again. Magellan was not one of them.

Magellan 1480-1521

FRANCIS DRAKE

A famous English seaman, Drake spent most of his life raiding Spain and Spanish possessions, often as a privateer (a kind of official pirate, licensed by the government). He was a brilliant navigator and a good leader. The reasons for his round-the-world voyage are mysterious, and Drake does not seem to have kept a log. He may have been told to look for an exit from the "North-West Passage" on the west coast of North America. But his main reason was probably plunder.

Drake 1543-1596

The *Golden Hind*
Drake sailed around the world from 1577 to 1580 in a ship called the *Golden Hind*. The ship was 23 m long and weighed 100 tonnes. The *Golden Hind* had about 12 cannon on board and was the largest of the five ships in Drake's fleet. In 1977 a replica of the ship was built to mark the 400th anniversary of Drake's voyage.

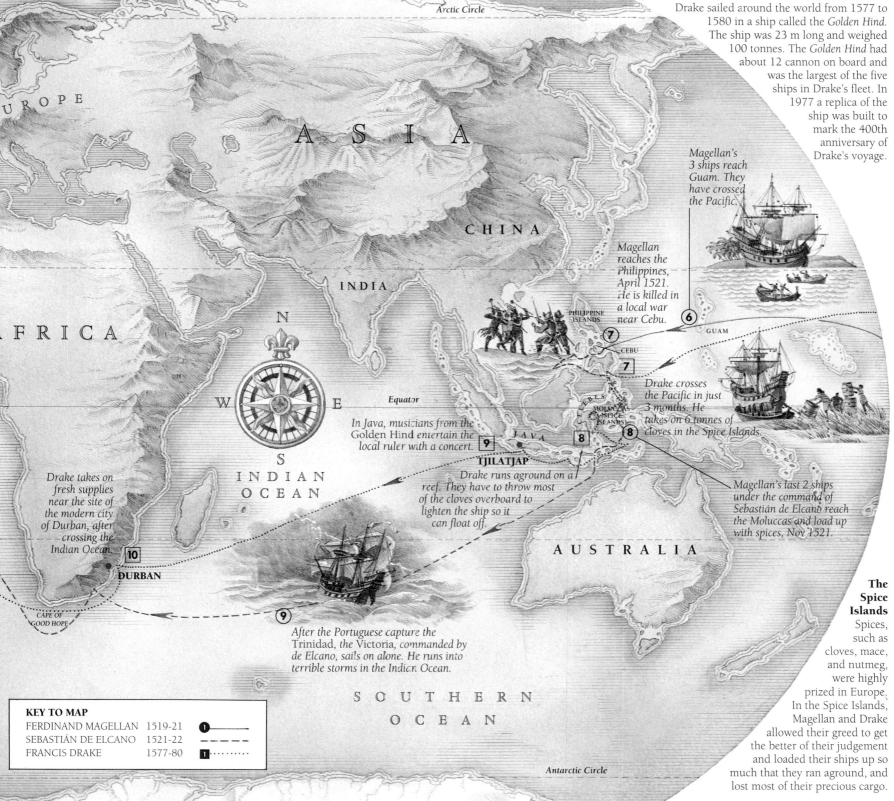

Magellan's 3 ships reach Guam. They have crossed the Pacific.

Magellan reaches the Philippines, April 1521. He is killed in a local war near Cebu.

Drake crosses the Pacific in just 3 months. He takes on 6 tonnes of cloves in the Spice Islands.

In Java, musicians from the Golden Hind entertain the local ruler with a concert.

Drake runs aground on a reef. They have to throw most of the cloves overboard to lighten the ship so it can float off.

Magellan's last 2 ships under the command of Sebastián de Elcano reach the Moluccas and load up with spices, Nov 1521.

Drake takes on fresh supplies near the site of the modern city of Durban, after crossing the Indian Ocean.

After the Portuguese capture the Trinidad, the Victoria, commanded by de Elcano, sails on alone. He runs into terrible storms in the Indian Ocean.

The Spice Islands
Spices, such as cloves, mace, and nutmeg, were highly prized in Europe. In the Spice Islands, Magellan and Drake allowed their greed to get the better of their judgement and loaded their ships up so much that they ran aground, and lost most of their precious cargo.

KEY TO MAP
FERDINAND MAGELLAN	1519-21	●———
SEBASTIÁN DE ELCANO	1521-22	●- - - -
FRANCIS DRAKE	1577-80	▣········

33

GOLD AND GLORY

THE SPANIARDS WHO FOLLOWED Columbus found new and thriving cultures in Central and South America. The Aztec people in Mexico and the Incas in Peru were highly sophisticated societies, although they were less technologically advanced than either Europeans or Asians. They had no iron tools, no ploughs or carts, and no horses, yet they had built magnificent stone cities, rich in treasure. This wealth turned out to be their ruin. Although the Aztecs held an empire of five million people, and the Incas one of more than six million, they were conquered by just a few hundred well-armed men.

The *conquistadores* (the Spanish name for "conquerors") and later the Portuguese *bandeirantes,* could not be controlled from Europe. The Spanish government had no plan to kill and conquer the people of Central and South America, but the adventurers were a long way from home and saw only the gold that would make them rich. Two Spaniards were responsible for leading the conquests of the Aztec and Inca Empires: Hernan Cortés and Francisco Pizarro.

Cortés lands at Veracruz, where he burns his ships as a sign that he will not be turning back.

MEXICO

MEXICO CITY (Tenochtitlán)

TLAXCALA

VERACRUZ

Cortés gathers allies at Tlaxcala and marches towards Tenochtitlán. Montezuma meets him outside the city.

The Spaniards land near the mouth of the Grijalva and trade with the local people.

HERNAN CORTÉS

Born to a noble Spanish family, Cortés studied law before going to the West Indies to seek his fortune. He became secretary to the governor, who put him in command of an expedition to Mexico in 1519. Within two years Cortés, a born leader and adventurer, had captured Mexico for Spain. He was helped by people from other civilizations who had been conquered by the Aztecs and were unhappy at the heavy taxes and slavery imposed by their Aztec rulers.

Cortés 1485-1547

Quetzalcoatl
The Aztec people believed that the Mexican god, Quetzalcoatl (left), would one day return. When Cortés invaded their land, many Aztecs thought he was Quetzalcoatl. This explains why the Aztecs and their emperor, Montezuma, were so trusting of Cortés at first.

Aztec knife
This ceremonial stone knife, a fine piece of Aztec craftwork, has a handle inlaid with turquoise. It was given to Cortés by the Aztecs. Knives such as this were used in Aztec ceremonies of human sacrifice.

Tenochtitlán
The beautiful Aztec city of Tenochtitlán was built on an island in a lake. This remarkable place was constructed of canals, aqueducts and bridges, buildings with terraces and hanging gardens, great stone temples, and palaces. Cortés led his army into Tenochtitlán then escaped from the city to get help. He joined up with 100,000 allies, who were rebelling against their Aztec rulers, and together they besieged the city. In 1521 the Aztec people, starving and dying of diseases they had caught from the Spaniards, surrendered to Cortés, who was declared lord of Mexico. The city of Tenochtitlán was destroyed (Cortés later rebuilt it as Mexico City), and the surviving Aztecs became slaves.

Cortés and Montezuma
When Cortés reached the Aztec capital Tenochtitlán, the emperor, Montezuma, arrived in style to meet him. They exchanged gifts, and the Spaniards were allowed to enter the city, but Montezuma was suspicious. The Spaniards soon started to take over, making him almost a prisoner in his own city. While Cortés was away from the city, trouble began and, by the time he returned, war had broken out. Montezuma was killed by his people, who believed he had betrayed them.

Pizarro c.1475-1541

FRANCISCO PIZARRO

The Spanish *conquistador*, Francisco Pizarro, went to Central America to seek his fortune. He crossed the Isthmus of Panama and reached the Pacific coast, where he heard stories of a rich country to the south. In 1531 he set out to conquer the Inca Empire. Nearly 60 years old, and with less than 200 men, in a few months he won control of the Inca Empire for Spain. Quarrels broke out among the Spaniards and Pizarro was later killed by his own soldiers.

Greed for gold
This pendant, made of gold, was the kind of treasure that the Spanish *conquistadores* wanted from the Aztec and Inca Empires. When the Inca, Atahualpa, was a prisoner of the Spaniards, he offered them a room filled to the ceiling with gold and silver in return for his freedom. The Spaniards accepted the ransom, but killed him anyway. Some years later, the Spaniards discovered rich gold and silver mines in Peru. They forced the Inca people to work as slaves in the mines, where they became sick and died in their thousands.

Battle at Cajamarca
In 1532 Pizarro and his men marched into Peru and crossed the Andes. At Cajamarca they met the Inca ruler Atahualpa, known simply as "the Inca". He greeted them peacefully. The Spaniards were nervous because they were surrounded by a huge Inca army. When a Spanish priest tried to explain Christianity to Atahualpa, the Inca threw the Bible aside. The Spaniards took this as an excuse to attack. They captured the Inca and killed his unarmed attendants. Later, when they no longer needed Atahualpa as a hostage, they killed him too.

CUBA

SANTIAGO

Cozumel Island

Chichén Itzá (temple-city)

YUCATÁN PENINSULA

Tikal (temple)

2 Cortés sails to the island of Cozumel, where his men scare away the people and plunder their villages for gold.

1 Cortés leaves Cuba with 11 ships and 500 men, Feb 1519. He sets sail for Mexico.

JAMAICA

CARIBBEAN SEA

THE BANDEIRANTES

The Portuguese colonists who came to Brazil settled on the coast. The only people who went far inland were Christian missionaries, and the *bandeirantes*. These were large bands of lawless men who lived mainly on the coast around São Paulo in the 17th century. Although they were more interested in money than exploration, these adventurers opened up much of Brazil for Europe. They made long journeys to the heart of the country for the purpose of capturing the local people to sell as slaves – a practice that was illegal. The discoveries that pleased them the most were the gold and diamonds they found in the region of Minas Gerais.

0   100   200   300 Kilometres

PACIFIC OCEAN

Pizarro leaves Panama, in 153?, in 2 ships with 170 men and horses, 2 small cannon and 3 muskets.

PANAMA

1

Lake Guatavita near Bogotá is linked to the legend of El Dorado ("the golden man"). According to legend, a local king was powdered daily with gold dust. Once a year he sailed out to the lake with gifts of gold for the gods. The Spaniards flocked here in the hope of finding gold.

Pizarro and his men land at Tumaco. Pizarro tells the local governor that he has come to rescue the people from the worship of idols.

2 TUMACO

Site of the legend of El Dorado

Magdalena

BOGOTÁ

Orinoco

SOUTH AMERICA

N W E S

Negro

ANDES MOUNTAINS

PUNÁ ISLAND

TUMBES

Marañón

PAITA

3

The Spaniards advance into the Inca Empire, heading for Cajamarca.

Pizarro and his men meet Atahualpa, at Cajamarca. They hold him hostage, accept a ransom, and then murder him.

CAJAMARCA **4**

Machu Picchu, the Inca city that Pizarro and his men never found. The ruins of this city in the Andes were only discovered in 1911.

Amazon

BRAZIL

Pizarro captures Cuzco
After the murder of Atahualpa, Pizarro and his men marched on to Cuzco, the Inca capital. A battle began and many of the Inca were slaughtered. The survivors had to bring out all the Inca treasures they had. These were melted down for gold. Pizarro used the gold to pay his men. The Spaniards then built their own capital city at Lima, near the coast, and from there they explored farther south and east. (One of Pizarro's men, Francisco de Orellana, sailed all the way down the River Amazon.)

The Spaniards enter the valley of Jauja where they meet hostile Indians whom they kill. The Spaniards build a settlement here.

PERU

JAUJA

LIMA

5

Apurímac

MACHU PICCHU

CUZCO **6** Pizarro and his army capture Cuzco, Nov 1533. After the battle they force the Incas to surrender their gold.

KEY TO MAP
HERNAN CORTÉS   1519-21   **1** ········
FRANCISCO PIZARRO   1531-33   **1** +++++

NEW EMPIRES

IN THE EARLY 16TH CENTURY, Europeans explored most of the east coast of North America, from Cape Breton to Florida. Like John Cabot a few years earlier, they were looking for a waterway that would take them to the Pacific Ocean. They still believed North America was a narrow land and that Asia was close by. But every sea passage, or strait, they explored turned out to be a river leading inland. The most hopeful discovery was the great Gulf of St Lawrence, explored in 1535 by Jacques Cartier's French expedition. It opened the way for the settlement of the St Lawrence valley by the French in the 17th century in what was then called Lower Canada.

Meanwhile, the Spaniards were exploring farther south. From their settlements in the Caribbean, they sailed to Florida and marched far inland. They discovered another great waterway, the Mississippi River, but no one realised that it was a useful "highway" into North America. In any case, the Spaniards were only interested in treasure. They were lured onwards, often to their deaths, by dreams and legends of golden cities waiting to be discovered.

A 16th-century map of the Americas
This map comes from an atlas of the world published in 1570. It gives quite an accurate picture of the "New World" (a name often given to North America after Columbus' arrival), which was completely unknown 80 years earlier. It shows the areas explored by the Spaniards and the St Lawrence River, but not the Great Lakes. In the south, the map shows the Magellan Strait dividing South America from the "southern continent".

PÁNFILO DE NARVÁEZ AND ÁLVAR NÚÑEZ CABEZA DE VACA

Pánfilo de Narváez was a Spanish *conquistador* who commanded an expedition to Florida in 1528. He reached the coast with 600 men and advanced inland a short way before being forced to return by hunger. Shipwreck, starvation, disease, and battles with the local people destroyed almost the whole company. One man who survived was Cabeza de Vaca. Shipwrecked in the Gulf of Mexico, he was saved by Yaqui tribesmen (right). Cabeza de Vaca, shown in the centre, lived with the tribes of the region for over five years.

HERNANDO DE SOTO

De Soto was a Spanish *conquistador*. He took over the job of conquering Florida after the disaster of the Narváez expedition. He had already made a fortune out of the conquest of the Incas in Peru, but he wanted more. Although Cabeza de Vaca told him there was no treasure to be found, de Soto thought he was lying and decided to find the treasure himself. For three years his expedition searched for gold that did not exist.

de Soto 1500-1542

Atrocities of de Soto
De Soto's expedition suffered extreme hardships, but also inflicted terrible cruelty on various native peoples, such as the Cherokee and Creek. He was instructed to treat them well unless they refused to accept the king of Spain and the Christian religion. But de Soto was only interested in gold and conquest. He was often well-received by the people he met and given gifts, such as strings of pearls. Yet he thought nothing of cutting off a man's head to see how sharp his sword was, and his cruelty soon turned the people of the region against him. His men even killed women and children.

NORTH AM

Cabeza de Vaca is amazed by the huge herds of hunch-backed, hairy "cows" on the plains. They are bison.

Cabeza de Vaca fords the Rio Grande. He continues his journey working as a trader and earns a reputation as a healer among local peoples.

4

EL PASO

Rio Grande

Pecos

3

2

Rio Grande

Cabeza de Vaca and 3 men escape from the Yaqui tribesmen after 5 years. They travel west.

PACIFIC

GULF OF CALIFORNIA

Sonora

SIERRA MADRE

CULIACÁN

5

OCEAN

Cabeza de Vaca reaches the Mexican coast, having walked about 2,000 km, 1536.

MEXICO

Cabeza de Vaca travels to Mexico City on a Spanish ship. He then goes to Veracruz.

0   100   200   300   400 Kilometres

6

MEXICO CITY

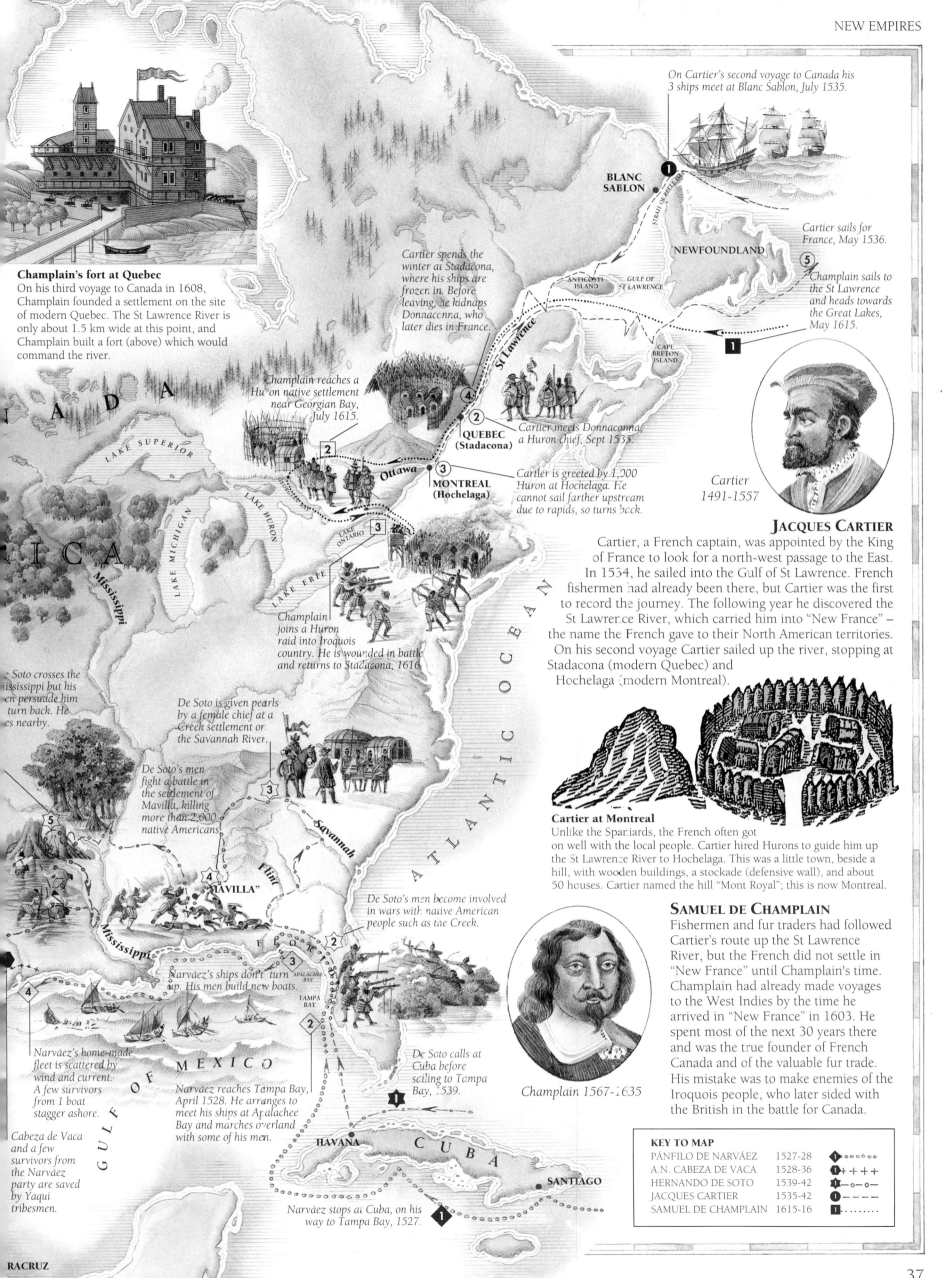

Champlain's fort at Quebec
On his third voyage to Canada in 1608, Champlain founded a settlement on the site of modern Quebec. The St Lawrence River is only about 1.5 km wide at this point, and Champlain built a fort (above) which would command the river.

On Cartier's second voyage to Canada his 3 ships meet at Blanc Sablon, July 1535.

BLANC SABLON

NEWFOUNDLAND

Cartier sails for France, May 1536.

⑤ *Champlain sails to the St Lawrence and heads towards the Great Lakes, May 1615.*

ANTICOSTI ISLAND   GULF OF ST LAWRENCE

CAPE BRETON ISLAND

Cartier spends the winter at Stadacona, where his ships are frozen in. Before leaving, he kidnaps Donnaconna, who later dies in France.

St Lawrence

④ *Cartier meets Donnaconna, a Huron chief, Sept 1535.*

QUEBEC (Stadacona)

Champlain reaches a Huron native settlement near Georgian Bay, July 1615.

②

Ottawa

③ MONTREAL (Hochelaga)

Cartier is greeted by 1,000 Huron at Hochelaga. He cannot sail farther upstream due to rapids, so turns back.

LAKE SUPERIOR

LAKE MICHIGAN

LAKE HURON

LAKE ONTARIO

③

LAKE ERIE

Champlain joins a Huron raid into Iroquois country. He is wounded in battle and returns to Stadacona, 1616.

Mississippi

CANADA

...ERICA

...e Soto crosses the ...ississippi but his ...en persuade him ...o turn back. He ...es nearby.

De Soto is given pearls by a female chief at a Creek settlement on the Savannah River.

De Soto's men fight a battle in the settlement of Mavilla, killing more than 2,000 native Americans.

⑤

③

Savannah

④ "MAVILLA"

Flint

②

FLORIDA

③

APALACHEE BAY

TAMPA BAY

②

Mississippi

④

Narváez's ships don't turn up. His men build new boats.

Narváez reaches Tampa Bay, April 1528. He arranges to meet his ships at Apalachee Bay and marches overland with some of his men.

Narváez's home-made fleet is scattered by wind and current. A few survivors from 1 boat stagger ashore.

Cabeza de Vaca and a few survivors from the Narváez party are saved by Yaqui tribesmen.

GULF OF MEXICO

De Soto's men become involved in wars with native American people such as the Creek.

ATLANTIC OCEAN

De Soto calls at Cuba before sailing to Tampa Bay, 1539.

①

HAVANA

CUBA

SANTIAGO

①

Narváez stops at Cuba, on his way to Tampa Bay, 1527.

...RACRUZ

Cartier 1491-1557

JACQUES CARTIER

Cartier, a French captain, was appointed by the King of France to look for a north-west passage to the East. In 1534, he sailed into the Gulf of St Lawrence. French fishermen had already been there, but Cartier was the first to record the journey. The following year he discovered the St Lawrence River, which carried him into "New France" – the name the French gave to their North American territories. On his second voyage Cartier sailed up the river, stopping at Stadacona (modern Quebec) and Hochelaga (modern Montreal).

Cartier at Montreal
Unlike the Spaniards, the French often got on well with the local people. Cartier hired Hurons to guide him up the St Lawrence River to Hochelaga. This was a little town, beside a hill, with wooden buildings, a stockade (defensive wall), and about 50 houses. Cartier named the hill "Mont Royal"; this is now Montreal.

SAMUEL DE CHAMPLAIN

Fishermen and fur traders had followed Cartier's route up the St Lawrence River, but the French did not settle in "New France" until Champlain's time. Champlain had already made voyages to the West Indies by the time he arrived in "New France" in 1603. He spent most of the next 30 years there and was the true founder of French Canada and of the valuable fur trade. His mistake was to make enemies of the Iroquois people, who later sided with the British in the battle for Canada.

Champlain 1567-1635

KEY TO MAP

PÁNFILO DE NARVÁEZ	1527-28	◆ ○○○○○
A.N. CABEZA DE VACA	1528-36	◆ +++
HERNANDO DE SOTO	1539-42	◆ -○-○-
JACQUES CARTIER	1535-42	● ----
SAMUEL DE CHAMPLAIN	1615-16	■ ....

ACROSS NORTH AMERICA

IN THE 17TH CENTURY the English founded colonies along the east coast of North America. Meanwhile, the French were active farther north, in the St Lawrence valley and the Great Lakes region. In 1672 a French Jesuit missionary, Father Marquette, reached the Mississippi River. This discovery opened up huge and rich new lands. In 1682 Robert Cavelier de la Salle sailed down the Mississippi to its mouth and claimed the entire territory for France, naming it "Louisiana" after his king, Louis XIV. Almost 100 years later the United States became an independent nation, although it still consisted of only a small area of land, lying between the Atlantic and the Mississippi. Louisiana, to the west, officially belonged to France, although the only people who lived there were the original native inhabitants. In 1803 the French sold this vast region to the United States. President Thomas Jefferson sent Meriwether Lewis and William Clark to explore it.

Lewis 1774-1809

Clark 1770-1838

LEWIS AND CLARK

President Jefferson chose his secretary Meriwether Lewis and Lewis's friend, William Clark, to lead an expedition to the newly acquired territory of Louisiana and to find a route to the Pacific coast. They set off up the Missouri from St Louis. They hoped it would lead them to the Columbia River in the north-west and eventually to the Pacific Ocean. They did not find an easy route to the Pacific, but were successful in other ways: they made friendly contact with many native peoples. They told them their new ruler lived in Washington, not France, and that there should be peace between their races.

The Mandans
Crossing the north-west of the United States, Lewis and Clark met various native tribes. Most were friendly, partly because Lewis and Clark had several native people with them. They spent the first winter in the country of the Mandan. The Mandan were farmers and hunters. They lived in large, round "lodges" made of logs, like this one. Some lodges held up to 20 families.

Lewis and Clark finally reach the Pacific coast, Dec 1805. They build a fort for the winter.

Lewis and Clark split up. Clark goes south. Lewis takes a more northern route and has to flee from the Blackfoot.

Lewis and Clark have to carry their canoes past rapids. A grizzly bear chases 6 men into the river.

Lewis and Clark meet where the Yellowstone joins the Missouri. They return to St Louis.

Lewis and Clark launch their canoes and paddle towards the Columbia River.

Lewis and Clark ride across the Rocky Mountains on horseback. The Shoshone guide them.

Lewis and Clark build a fort beside a Mandan settlement and spend the winter there.

FORT CLATSOP

Columbia

Snake

GREAT FALLS

THREE FORKS

Yellowstone

FORT MANDAN

PACIFIC OCEAN

Plat

NOR AMEI

Up the Missouri
Lewis and Clark used canoes like those made by the native peoples for their expedition up the Missouri. As they went they found that the river grew narrower and the current stronger. Sometimes they had to leave their oars and pull the canoes upstream from the river bank using ropes. Sometimes they dragged their canoes overland on a rough wagon. "So far", wrote Lewis, "we have experienced more difficulty from the navigation of the Missouri than danger from the savages."

KEY TO MAP
ROBERT CAVELIER DE LA SALLE		
1st journey	1678-80	+++++
2nd journey	1680-82	·········
LEWIS & CLARK	1804-06	·········
MERIWETHER LEWIS	1806	+ + + + +
WILLIAM CLARK	1806	o− o− o− o− o

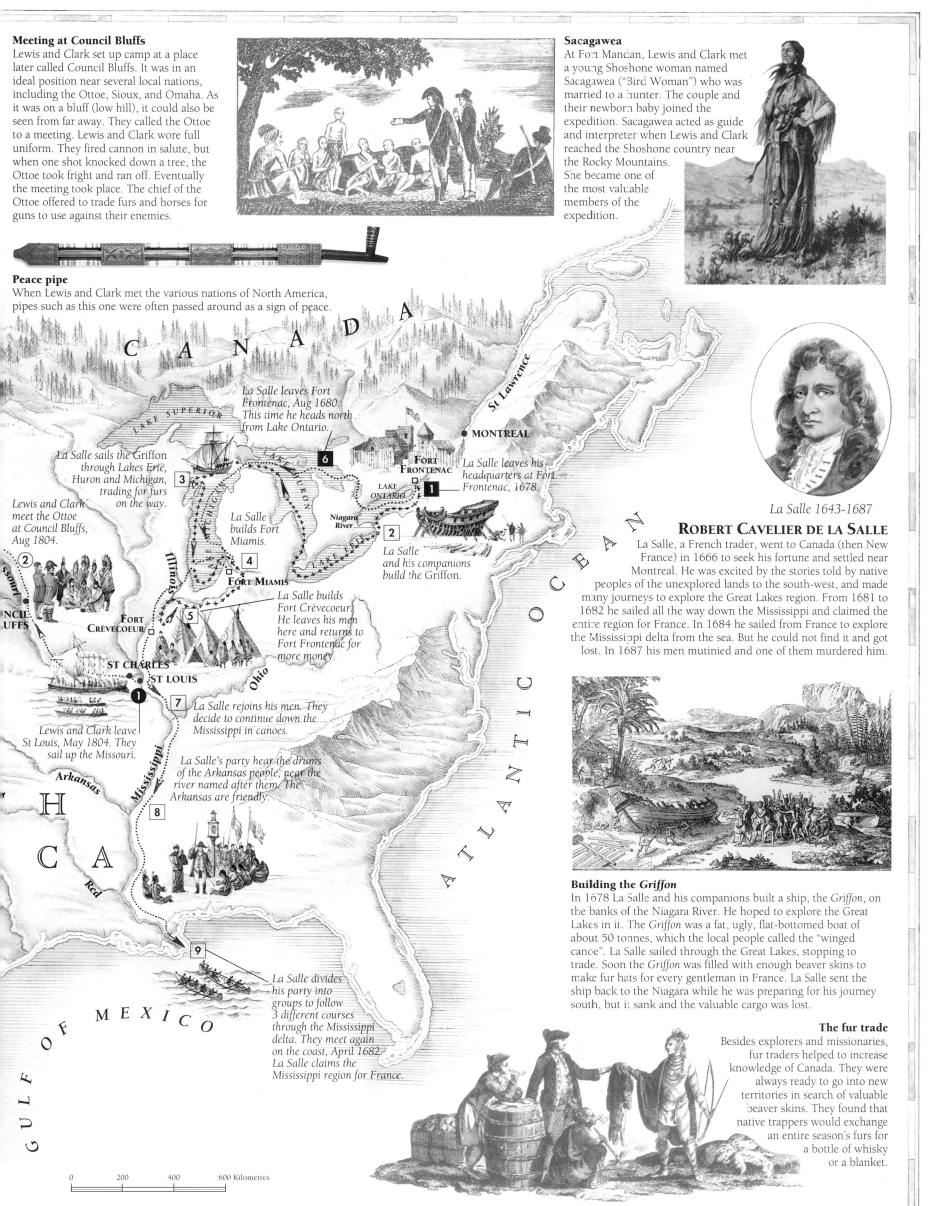

Meeting at Council Bluffs
Lewis and Clark set up camp at a place later called Council Bluffs. It was in an ideal position near several local nations, including the Ottoe, Sioux, and Omaha. As it was on a bluff (low hill), it could also be seen from far away. They called the Ottoe to a meeting. Lewis and Clark wore full uniform. They fired cannon in salute, but when one shot knocked down a tree, the Ottoe took fright and ran off. Eventually the meeting took place. The chief of the Ottoe offered to trade furs and horses for guns to use against their enemies.

Peace pipe
When Lewis and Clark met the various nations of North America, pipes such as this one were often passed around as a sign of peace.

Sacagawea
At Fort Mandan, Lewis and Clark met a young Shoshone woman named Sacagawea ("Bird Woman") who was married to a hunter. The couple and their newborn baby joined the expedition. Sacagawea acted as guide and interpreter when Lewis and Clark reached the Shoshone country near the Rocky Mountains. She became one of the most valuable members of the expedition.

La Salle 1643-1687

ROBERT CAVELIER DE LA SALLE
La Salle, a French trader, went to Canada (then New France) in 1666 to seek his fortune and settled near Montreal. He was excited by the stories told by native peoples of the unexplored lands to the south-west, and made many journeys to explore the Great Lakes region. From 1681 to 1682 he sailed all the way down the Mississippi and claimed the entire region for France. In 1684 he sailed from France to explore the Mississippi delta from the sea. But he could not find it and got lost. In 1687 his men mutinied and one of them murdered him.

La Salle leaves Fort Frontenac, Aug 1680. This time he heads north from Lake Ontario.

La Salle sails the Griffon through Lakes Erie, Huron and Michigan, trading for furs on the way.

Lewis and Clark meet the Ottoe at Council Bluffs, Aug 1804.

La Salle builds Fort Miamis.

La Salle leaves his headquarters at Fort Frontenac, 1678.

La Salle and his companions build the Griffon.

La Salle builds Fort Crèvecoeur. He leaves his men here and returns to Fort Frontenac for more money.

Lewis and Clark leave St Louis, May 1804. They sail up the Missouri.

La Salle rejoins his men. They decide to continue down the Mississippi in canoes.

La Salle's party hear the drums of the Arkansas people, near the river named after them. The Arkansas are friendly.

La Salle divides his party into groups to follow 3 different courses through the Mississippi delta. They meet again on the coast, April 1682. La Salle claims the Mississippi region for France.

Building the *Griffon*
In 1678 La Salle and his companions built a ship, the *Griffon*, on the banks of the Niagara River. He hoped to explore the Great Lakes in it. The *Griffon* was a fat, ugly, flat-bottomed boat of about 50 tonnes, which the local people called the "winged canoe". La Salle sailed through the Great Lakes, stopping to trade. Soon the *Griffon* was filled with enough beaver skins to make fur hats for every gentleman in France. La Salle sent the ship back to the Niagara while he was preparing for his journey south, but it sank and the valuable cargo was lost.

The fur trade
Besides explorers and missionaries, fur traders helped to increase knowledge of Canada. They were always ready to go into new territories in search of valuable beaver skins. They found that native trappers would exchange an entire season's furs for a bottle of whisky or a blanket.

0   200   400   600 Kilometres

THE HEART OF ASIA

IN THE 16TH CENTURY Europeans knew very little about the huge continent of Asia. They did not even know if Cathay, described by Marco Polo in the 13th century, was the same place as China, the coast of which was known to Portuguese sailors. European travellers did not "discover" Asia, as Columbus "discovered" America, and they could not set up colonies. They had definite reasons for their journeys but, for the most part, they travelled as guests – and not always welcome guests.

Europeans made extraordinary journeys in central and eastern Asia. Among these travellers were the Jesuits – Roman Catholic missionary priests who belonged to the Society of Jesus. St Francis Xavier was the first European to visit parts of Japan, Father Matteo Ricci reached Peking, and de Goes, Andrade, Grueber, and d'Orville crossed great mountain ranges in search of groups of Christians.

Matteo Ricci in China

Father Matteo Ricci (1552-1610) was an Italian missionary in India. He learned Chinese and was allowed to settle in Canton in 1583. He dressed as a Chinese, and taught Christianity as a way of life, not as the only true religion. This made it more acceptable to the Chinese. After years of trying, Ricci was invited to Peking to meet the emperor in 1600. He presented a clock to the emperor, who was so pleased that he ordered a building to house it.

BENTO DE GOES

A Portuguese from the Azores, de Goes was a professional soldier before he joined the Jesuits in India. He worked with St Francis Xavier as a missionary in Lahore, and acted as ambassador between the Portuguese in Goa and the court of Akbar the Great, the Mughal emperor in India. In 1601 he was chosen to lead an expedition to Cathay, to look for Christian peoples who were thought to live between Cathay and India.

de Goes 1562-1607

Andrade 1580-1634

ANTONIO DE ANDRADE

Father Andrade was a Portuguese Jesuit missionary in India, who was inspired by the journey of Bento de Goes. He was determined to follow in his footsteps. Disguised as a Hindu pilgrim, and sometimes travelling with only one companion, he made his way into western Tibet, becoming the first European to cross the Himalayas. He returned to India by the same route, but four years later made the journey again and founded a Jesuit mission in Tsaparang.

De Goes and Isaac are delayed for a year at Yarkand. They visit Khotan and watch miners collecting precious stones. **4**

De Goes is captured by 4 bandits. He escapes while they fight over his hat, which contains jewels. **3**

Andrade visits the Hindu temple of Badrinath with the pilgrims. He crosses the Himalayas, sometimes on bridges made of frozen snow.

Grueber and d'Orville cross the mountains into Tibet through a pass 5,000 m above sea level. They change from horses to yaks.

TIEN SHAN

HAMI

KORLA

YARKAND

PAMIRS

HINDU KUSH

KHOTAN

KABUL

PESHAWAR

TIBET

At Lahore de Goes and Isaac join the annual caravan to Peshawar and Kabul. They cross the Hindu Kush (mountains).

LAHORE **2**

"TSAPARANG" **2**

BADRINATH

LHASA **3**

DELHI **1**

Indus

AGRA **1**

KATHMANDU

H I M A L A Y A S

Brahmaputra

Andrade sets out for Tibet in 1624. He travels with the emperor as far as Delhi, then joins a pilgrim caravan.

5

4

Grueber and d'Orville reach Agra. They have travelled from Peking to Agra in 11 months. D'Orville dies here. Grueber returns to Europe.

PATNA

Grueber and d'Orville reach Kathmandu, where the king is about to fight a battle. They give the king a telescope. When he looks through it, he thinks the enemy has suddenly advanced.

Grueber and d'Orville reach Lhasa, Oct 1661. They are the first Europeans to give an eyewitness report of this legendary "forbidden city".

De Goes leaves the Mughal court in 1602, under the name of Bandar Abdullah. He travels with a friend, a man named Isaac.

A R A B I A N   S E A

I N D I A

Irrawaddy

Francis Xavier arrives in Goa, 1542. In the next 5 years he travels all over India and Sri Lanka.

1 GOA

BAY OF BENGAL

KEY TO MAP

FRANCIS XAVIER	1541-52	
BENTO DE GOES	1602-07	
ANTONIO DE ANDRADE	1624-26	
GRUEBER AND D'ORVILLE	1661-64	

0   200   400   600 Kilometres

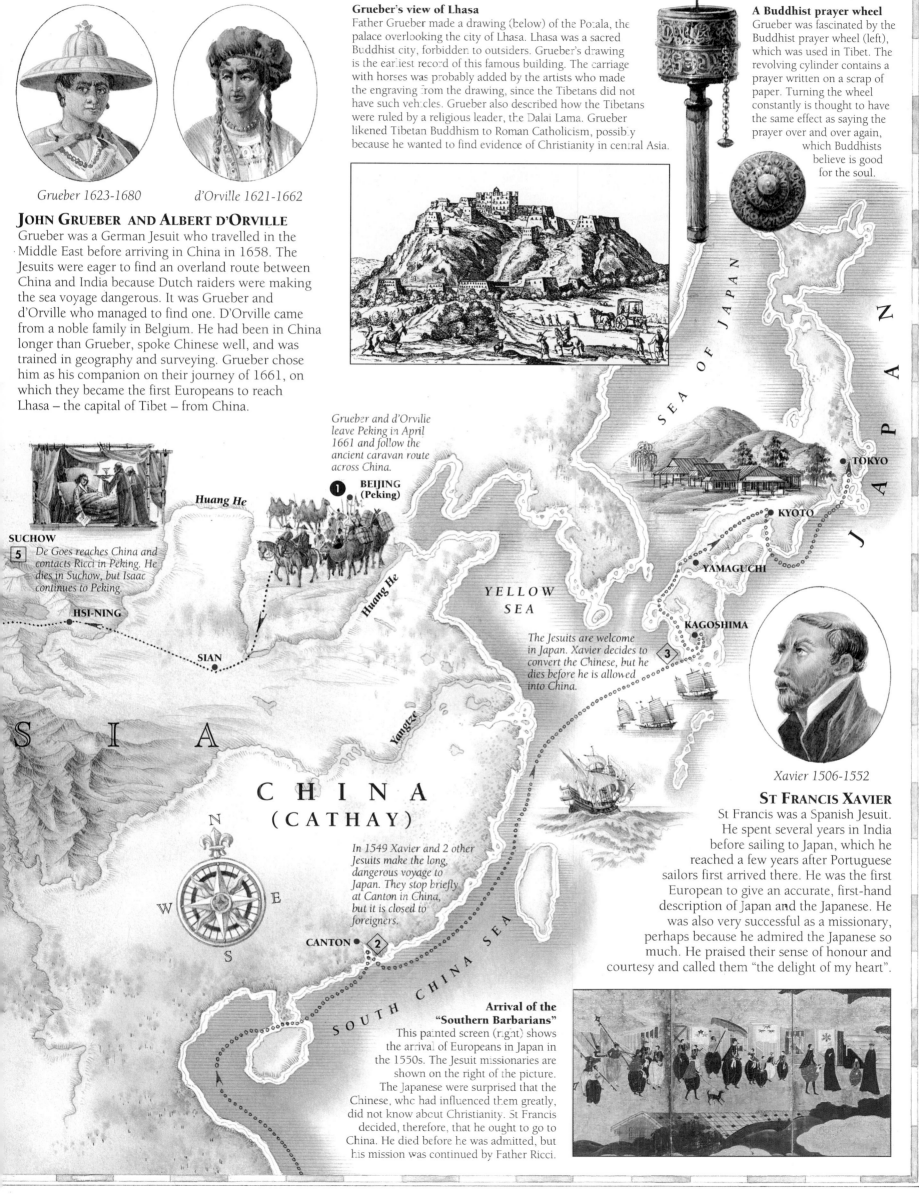

Grueber's view of Lhasa
Father Grueber made a drawing (below) of the Potala, the palace overlooking the city of Lhasa. Lhasa was a sacred Buddhist city, forbidden to outsiders. Grueber's drawing is the earliest record of this famous building. The carriage with horses was probably added by the artists who made the engraving from the drawing, since the Tibetans did not have such vehicles. Grueber also described how the Tibetans were ruled by a religious leader, the Dalai Lama. Grueber likened Tibetan Buddhism to Roman Catholicism, possibly because he wanted to find evidence of Christianity in central Asia.

A Buddhist prayer wheel
Grueber was fascinated by the Buddhist prayer wheel (left), which was used in Tibet. The revolving cylinder contains a prayer written on a scrap of paper. Turning the wheel constantly is thought to have the same effect as saying the prayer over and over again, which Buddhists believe is good for the soul.

Grueber 1623-1680   *d'Orville 1621-1662*

JOHN GRUEBER AND ALBERT D'ORVILLE

Grueber was a German Jesuit who travelled in the Middle East before arriving in China in 1658. The Jesuits were eager to find an overland route between China and India because Dutch raiders were making the sea voyage dangerous. It was Grueber and d'Orville who managed to find one. D'Orville came from a noble family in Belgium. He had been in China longer than Grueber, spoke Chinese well, and was trained in geography and surveying. Grueber chose him as his companion on their journey of 1661, on which they became the first Europeans to reach Lhasa – the capital of Tibet – from China.

Grueber and d'Orville leave Peking in April 1661 and follow the ancient caravan route across China.

SUCHOW
5 *De Goes reaches China and contacts Ricci in Peking. He dies in Suchow, but Isaac continues to Peking.*

HSI-NING

SIAN

Huang He

Huang He

① BEIJING (Peking)

YELLOW SEA

The Jesuits are welcome in Japan. Xavier decides to convert the Chinese, but he dies before he is allowed into China.

③

TOKYO

KYOTO

YAMAGUCHI

KAGOSHIMA

SEA OF JAPAN

J A P A N

Yangtze

A S I A

C H I N A (CATHAY)

In 1549 Xavier and 2 other Jesuits make the long, dangerous voyage to Japan. They stop briefly at Canton in China, but it is closed to foreigners.

CANTON ②

SOUTH CHINA SEA

Xavier 1506-1552

ST FRANCIS XAVIER

St Francis was a Spanish Jesuit. He spent several years in India before sailing to Japan, which he reached a few years after Portuguese sailors first arrived there. He was the first European to give an accurate, first-hand description of Japan and the Japanese. He was also very successful as a missionary, perhaps because he admired the Japanese so much. He praised their sense of honour and courtesy and called them "the delight of my heart".

Arrival of the "Southern Barbarians"
This painted screen (right) shows the arrival of Europeans in Japan in the 1550s. The Jesuit missionaries are shown on the right of the picture. The Japanese were surprised that the Chinese, who had influenced them greatly, did not know about Christianity. St Francis decided, therefore, that he ought to go to China. He died before he was admitted, but his mission was continued by Father Ricci.

THE PACIFIC EXPLORERS

FERDINAND MAGELLAN'S EXPEDITION across the Pacific made Europe aware of the vastness of the ocean on the far side of the world. But his voyage had another effect. Europeans became curious to find out if there really was a huge continent in the South Pacific. Over the next 250 years several explorers tried to find out, but curiosity was not their only motive. They were also driven on by the three great European causes: preaching, profit and power.

In 1567 the South American Álvaro de Mendaña sailed west from Lima with several Franciscan friars. His aims were to convert the people of the Pacific to Christianity, search for gold and treasure, and establish a Spanish settlement. His discovery of the Solomon Islands was the first step in an adventure of exploration which the Englishman James Cook was to complete two centuries later.

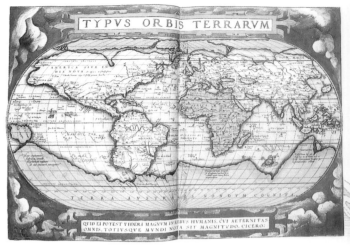

The southern continent
Legends of a great land to the south stirred the imaginations of even the earliest map-makers. The Greek geographer Ptolemy (AD 90-168) thought the Indian Ocean was surrounded by land. By 1570, when the 16th-century Flemish geographer Abraham Ortelius drew his map (above), the southern continent was a little better defined, and was named Terra Australis.

The Solomon Islands, discovered by Álvaro de Mendaña in 1568.

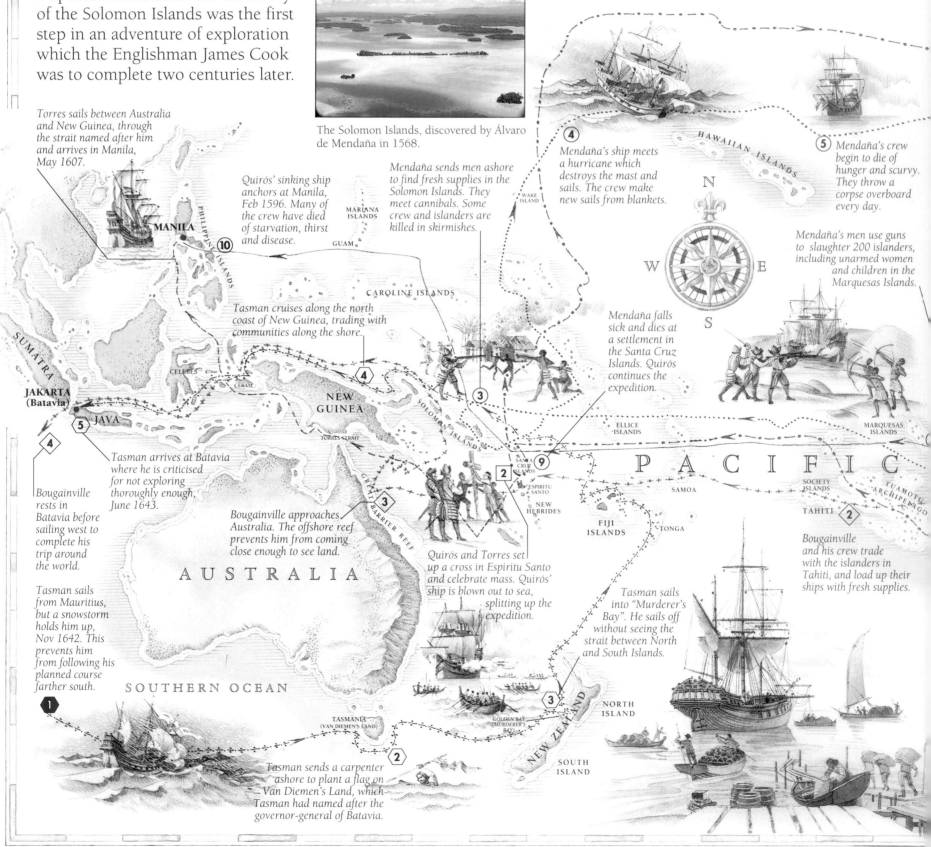

Torres sails between Australia and New Guinea, through the strait named after him and arrives in Manila, May 1607.

Quirós' sinking ship anchors at Manila, Feb 1596. Many of the crew have died of starvation, thirst and disease.

Mendaña sends men ashore to find fresh supplies in the Solomon Islands. They meet cannibals. Some crew and islanders are killed in skirmishes.

Mendaña's ship meets a hurricane which destroys the mast and sails. The crew make new sails from blankets.

Mendaña's crew begin to die of hunger and scurvy. They throw a corpse overboard every day.

Mendaña's men use guns to slaughter 200 islanders, including unarmed women and children in the Marquesas Islands.

Tasman cruises along the north coast of New Guinea, trading with communities along the shore.

Mendaña falls sick and dies at a settlement in the Santa Cruz Islands. Quirós continues the expedition.

Tasman arrives at Batavia where he is criticised for not exploring thoroughly enough, June 1643.

Bougainville rests in Batavia before sailing west to complete his trip around the world.

Bougainville approaches Australia. The offshore reef prevents him from coming close enough to see land.

Quirós and Torres set up a cross in Espiritu Santo and celebrate mass. Quirós' ship is blown out to sea, splitting up the expedition.

Bougainville and his crew trade with the islanders in Tahiti, and load up their ships with fresh supplies.

Tasman sails from Mauritius, but a snowstorm holds him up, Nov 1642. This prevents him from following his planned course farther south.

Tasman sails into "Murderer's Bay". He sails off without seeing the strait between North and South Islands.

Tasman sends a carpenter ashore to plant a flag on Van Diemen's Land, which Tasman had named after the governor-general of Batavia.

MANILA
PHILIPPINE ISLANDS
MARIANA ISLANDS
GUAM
CAROLINE ISLANDS
WAKE ISLAND
HAWAIIAN ISLANDS
SUMATRA
JAKARTA (Batavia)
JAVA
CELEBES
CERAM
NEW GUINEA
TORRES STRAIT
GREAT BARRIER REEF
SOLOMON ISLANDS
SANTA CRUZ ISLANDS
ESPIRITU SANTO
NEW HEBRIDES
ELLICE ISLANDS
SAMOA
FIJI ISLANDS
TONGA
SOCIETY ISLANDS
TAHITI
TUAMOTU ARCHIPELAGO
MARQUESAS ISLANDS
PACIFIC
AUSTRALIA
SOUTHERN OCEAN
TASMANIA (VAN DIEMEN'S LAND)
GOLDEN BAY (MURDERER'S BAY)
NORTH ISLAND
SOUTH ISLAND
NEW ZEALAND

ÁLVARO DE MENDAÑA

Spaniard Álvaro de Mendaña was just 25 years old when his ship, the *Los Reyes*, set sail from Callao, Peru, in 1567. The voyage lasted two years. The explorers got lost, and suffered starvation, thirst, disease, and hurricanes. But Mendaña and his captain, Pedro de Sarmiento, discovered the Solomon Islands on this first trip. Many years later, in 1595, Mendaña set out again with a Portuguese pilot, Pedro Fernández de Quirós. His aim was to start a colony, so Mendaña took 378 settlers with him. The trip was a complete disaster, leading eventually to the death of Mendaña and many of the crew.

Mendaña 1541-1595

QUIRÓS AND TORRES

One of the survivors of Mendaña's 1595 expedition was Pedro Fernández de Quirós (1565-1614). He sailed the Pacific again in 1605, in command of three ships and 300 men. They visited the Cook Islands and the New Hebrides (left), landing on Espiritu Santo. Quirós became ill and, when his ship was separated from the rest of the expedition, Luis Váez de Torres took command. Torres sailed around New Guinea, proving that it is an island.

The Dutch East India Company

From the start of the 17th century the powerful Dutch East India Company controlled all Dutch trade in the Pacific, and Indian, Ocean. Its aims in the Pacific were trade and profit. Exploration was usually unplanned. Dutch ships sailing to the company's headquarters in Batavia (now Jakarta) were frequently blown off course. So the Dutch learned about Australia's west coast by accident. A few deliberate expeditions added details to their knowledge of the south and north. In 1615 a Dutch expedition led by Jakob Le Maire and Willem Corneliszoon Schouten crossed the Pacific from Cape Horn to Batavia, calling at a number of island groups on the way.

ABEL JANSZOON TASMAN

Dutch knowledge of the southern continent grew between 1642 and 1644 following the voyages of Abel Tasman of the Dutch East India Company. The governor-general of Batavia sent Tasman on his first expedition with the aim of sailing east from the Indian Ocean, to the Pacific. In the course of his voyage, Tasman discovered Van Diemen's Land (now Tasmania), saw New Zealand, and the Fiji Islands and Tonga.

Tasman 1603-1659

N O R T H A M E R I C A

Mendaña's damaged ships land at Lower California and then limp down the coast to Callao, Sept 1569.

ACAPULCO

③

Quirós and his crew, living on rainwater and fish, sail east. They return to Acapulco nearly a year after they left.

Mendaña's expedition sails between the Marquesas and low-lying Tuamotu island groups without ever sighting land.

Mendaña and Quirós set sail from Peru in a fleet of 4 ships, April 1595.

⑦ **PAITA**

O C E A N

S O U T H A M E R I C A

②

CALLAO ● **LIMA**
①

①

Quirós and Torres set sail in charge of 3 ships and 300 men, Dec 1605.

Mendaña leaves Callao, Nov 1567. A day later the ship hits a sleeping whale.

Murderer's Bay
Tasman's visit to New Zealand was brief and unpleasant. His ships anchored in a bay on the north coast of what is now called South Island, where they were greeted by groups of native people – the Maori – in canoes. The Maoris seemed friendly at first but, when the Dutch rowed a small boat between their ships, they attacked, killing four men. Tasman called the anchorage "Murderer's Bay", and sailed away from New Zealand without landing.

LOUIS BOUGAINVILLE

Bougainville, a Frenchman, explored the Pacific as part of a trip that began in 1766. Sailing north-west from the Strait of Magellan, he visited the islands of Tuamotu and Tahiti, continuing through the Samoan and New Hebrides islands. He would have reached Australia, but dared not cross the Great Barrier Reef that guards the continent's north-east coast. Instead, he sailed north of New Guinea and on to Batavia.

Bougainville 1729-1811

Bougainville sets sail in 1766. He sails through the Strait of Magellan and into the Pacific in his ship Boudeuse in Jan 1768.

A T L A N T I C O C E A N

KEY TO MAP		
ÁLVARO DE MENDAÑA	1567-69	① ·········
MENDAÑA (with Quirós)	1595-96	② ———
QUIRÓS (with Torres)	1605-06	① –o–o–
LUIS VÁEZ DE TORRES	1606-07	
ABEL JANSZOON TASMAN	1642-43	① –·–·–
LOUIS BOUGAINVILLE	1766-69	① ⊤⊤⊤

①
FALKLAND ISLANDS

STRAIT OF MAGELLAN *CAPE HORN*

0   500   1000   1500 Kilometres

COOK IN THE SOUTH SEAS

IN THE 18TH CENTURY, Europeans knew very little about the South Pacific. Many did not believe it was an ocean at all and thought instead that the region contained a giant southern continent, which stretched across the South Pole and reached as far north as the tropics. The Solomon Islands, New Zealand, and possibly even Australia were all considered part of this huge land mass. Two nations – Great Britain and France – took the lead in exploring the South Pacific, but it was an Englishman, Captain James Cook, who solved the mystery of the southern continent for ever. Cook made three voyages to the South Seas between 1768 and 1779. His charts of the region, showing the Solomon Islands, New Zealand's North and South Islands, and the east coast of Australia, proved they were separate countries rather than a single continent. He never saw Antarctica, but he sailed close enough to realize that this was the true southern continent.

Cook goes ashore to take possession of the land he has found.

⑨

The Endeavour runs aground on the Great Barrier Reef causing a large hole that has to be repaired.

⑧

GREAT BARRIER REEF

Cook and his men survey the coast in one of the ship's boats. The few Aborigines they see run off.

⑦

SOUTH PACIFIC OCEAN

N E S W

AUSTRALIA

BOTANY BAY

⑥

At Botany Bay, Joseph Banks and the other naturalists collect hundreds of plants they have never seen before.

Cook first sees Australia. He names the area Point Hicks after the officer who first sighted it.

⑤

POINT HICKS

0 100 200 300 400 Kilometres

An unusual choice of ship

Cook learned to be a skilled seaman by shipping coal around the North Sea from his home town, the port of Whitby. Later, when he had to choose a ship to sail around the world, he chose a Whitby collier and renamed it the *Endeavour*. Colliers were built to carry coal, so the *Endeavour* was neither beautiful nor fast, but she was tough. There was enough room on board for stores and a crew of 94 men, including the wealthy young naturalist, Joseph Banks and his team of scientists.

CAPTAIN JAMES COOK

Cook joined the Royal Navy in 1755 at the age of 27, after serving 10 years in merchant ships. Although he joined the Navy at a low level, he was a skilled navigator and pilot and gained rapid promotion. However, he did not become an officer until 1768, when he was appointed to lead the expedition to the Pacific.

Cook 1728-1779

The kangaroo

Cook's crew were the first Europeans to see an Australian kangaroo. They were totally confused by it and couldn't decide what kind of animal it might be. It was the colour of a mouse, the size of a deer and it jumped like a hare. In the end they decided it must be "some kind of stag".

TASMANIA

Queen Charlotte Sound, a collection of fine harbours, visited by Cook on all his voyages to New Zealand.

Cook and his crew are attacked by Maori. They shoot back and, to Cook's distress, several Maori are killed.

②

NEW ZEALAND

NORTH ISLAND

QUEEN CHARLOTTE SOUND

Coo arriv in Ne Zealan Oct 176

③

COOK STRAIT

CAPE TURNAGAIN

Cook and his crew trade with the Maori.

Storms blow Cook off course, but he fights his way back, determined that his map of the coastline will be accurate.

④

SOUTH ISLAND

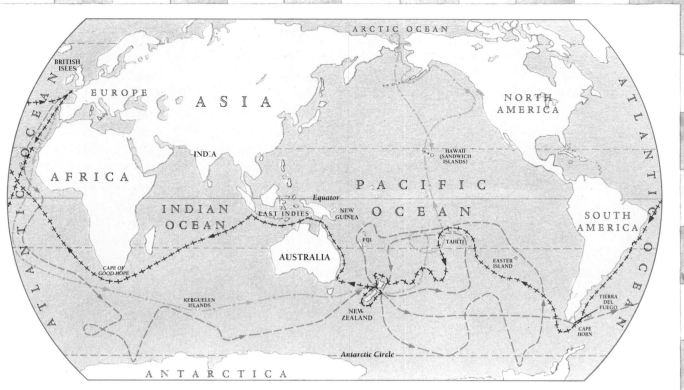

Around the world (1768-1779)

James Cook made three voyages from the British Isles to the South Seas. This map shows the complete routes. On his first voyage, in 1768, he sailed to Tahiti, New Zealand and the east coast of Australia; on the second, in 1772, he sailed due south into Antarctic waters, and guessed correctly that there was an area of frozen land around the South Pole. On his third voyage, in 1776, he sailed to the North Pacific looking for an inlet that would lead him to the Arctic Ocean. On the way, he found Hawaii by chance.

The beauty of Tahiti

Cook sailed to Tahiti on his first voyage. After the harsh climate of Tierra del Fuego, where two of Banks's companions froze to death looking for plants, the lush beauty of the island seemed like paradise. The people were friendly and the exotic plants and wildlife delighted Banks and the other naturalists. They tried new foods, such as this breadfruit (left), painted by Sydney Parkinson, an artist on the *Endeavour*. It is a white fibrous fruit, but it doesn't taste much like bread, in spite of its name.

Medical care

A medicine chest like this one (left) would have been carried by the ship's surgeon. It contained various tonics, but unfortunately no cure for the high fevers that killed many of Cook's crew in the East Indies.

Trading with the Maori

Cook and his crew first landed on New Zealand's North Island in 1769. At first they found the people there, the Maori, hostile, but after this bad beginning Cook won their trust. The Maori enjoyed trading with the crew and would exchange fruit for beads or ship's cloth for lobsters (right). Cook described the Maori as strong, active, artistic, brave, honest people who were warlike, but not treacherous.

A healthy crew

Cook took great care of his men's health, making sure that their diet contained fresh meat and vegetables whenever possible. As a result, scurvy – a disease caused by lack of vitamins, and the greatest menace on long voyages – was almost unknown on Cook's ships. He once had a man flogged for not eating properly. He insisted on keeping the ship spotless, believing that dirt spreads disease. Anyone who did fall ill was treated by the ship's surgeon. One of the remedies he used was the antimony cup, shown above right. Antimony is a metallic mixture, which was used to line the cup. When wine was poured into the cup, it reacted with the antimony. Ill members of the crew were given wine in it to make them sick. This was thought to reduce fever.

Cook's chronometer

Cook took this chronometer, or ship's clock (below), with him on his second voyage. It was the first timepiece able to keep going during a voyage round the world, enabling Cook to measure longitude (distance east-west) accurately. At the end of the voyage the chronometer showed an error of only 13 km.

Approaching Antarctica

On his second voyage, Cook crossed the Antarctic Circle twice. He never actually saw Antarctica, the real southern continent, though he was very close to it several times. "Ice mountains", as he called the icebergs, prevented him from sailing closer to it. His crew chipped chunks of ice from the icebergs to use as drinking water. Cook felt sure the ice stretched all the way to the South Pole, and wrote in his journal that he could think of no reason why any man should want to sail in these cold and dangerous waters again.

Cook dies in Hawaii

On his third voyage, Cook came across the Hawaiian Islands, which he named the Sandwich Islands. He spent the winter there getting to know the islands and their inhabitants, who were very friendly. In spring he left to explore the coast of North America, but had to return to Hawaii to repair a broken mast. This time the islanders did not welcome the strangers so warmly, perhaps because they were short of food. A quarrel began when some of the islanders stole one of the ship's boats. A short scuffle broke out on the beach and Cook was stabbed to death.

ACROSS AUSTRALIA

THE FIRST BRITISH COLONISTS arrived in Australia in 1788, 10 years after Captain Cook's crew left. They were mostly convicts, sent there instead of prison, and their guards, but others soon followed. The first town arose on the site of modern Sydney.

For many years, no one travelled even as far as the Blue Mountains, only 65 km away, but as settlement increased, people went out in search of new grazing land and explored the country further. Some followed the great rivers of the south-east, the Murray and the Darling, then crossed the Great Dividing Range and pushed north; others set out to link the growing number of towns in the south. Yet by the 1840s the heart of Australia was still a mystery. Some people thought it contained a great inland sea; others suspected it was nothing but desert. The extreme heat and drought defeated many who tried to reach the centre. In 1859, the South Australian government offered a prize to the first person who could cross the continent from south to north. By 1860 the race was on.

Stuart 1815-1866

JOHN McDOUALL STUART

Stuart was born in Scotland. As a young man he emigrated to Australia and worked as a surveyor, a farmer, and then as a gold prospector. He got to know the country quite well. In 1845 he joined an expedition led by Charles Sturt and discovered Cooper's Creek. By the time he set out to cross the continent in 1860, he was already an experienced explorer. He knew how to survive on a diet of flour, mice, and thistles.

Stuart completes the journey across the continent on his third attempt, July 1862. He reaches the coast and dips his tired feet in the sea.

DARWIN

ADELAIDE RIVER

DALY WATERS

Stuart abandons his first attempt to cross the continent when Aborigines set fire to the bush ahead of him.

TENNANT CREEK

Stuart reaches the centre of Australia on his first attempt to cross it. He raises a flag on a hill, later known as Mount Stuart.

ALICE SPRINGS

AUSTRA

The intense heat of the Simpson Desert prevented Charles Sturt's expedition from reaching the centre of Australia in 1845.

Fortescue

Ashburton

Gascoyne

Murchison

Eyre and his companions dig down nearly 3 m to find water.

Eyre and his last companion, Wylie, are half dead from starvation when they shoot a kangaroo.

PERTH

CEDUNA

STREA BA

GREAT AUSTRALIAN BIG

ALBANY

Eyre reaches Albany in July 1841.

Stuart crosses the continent.

John Stuart set out to cross Australia from Adelaide in March 1860. He took just one companion and reached the centre of the continent by April, but near Tennant Creek, hostile Aborigines barred his way and he had to turn back. On Stuart's second attempt, he almost reached Daly Waters, but miles of thorny bushes blocked his path. His third attempt was successful. This time, he took 10 men with him, leaving Adelaide in October 1861. He reached the coast near present-day Darwin in July 1862 and raised the flag in triumph (left). However, he was unaware that farther east his rival in the race, Burke, had already beaten him to it.

Eyre 1815-1901

EDWARD EYRE

Eyre, an Englishman, went to Australia in 1832, aged 17. He worked as an "overlander", driving herds of cattle across country and found the lake and peninsula now named after him. He used Aborigines as guides. In 1840 an Aborigine named Wylie joined him on the tough expedition to look for a route to link Adelaide and Albany.

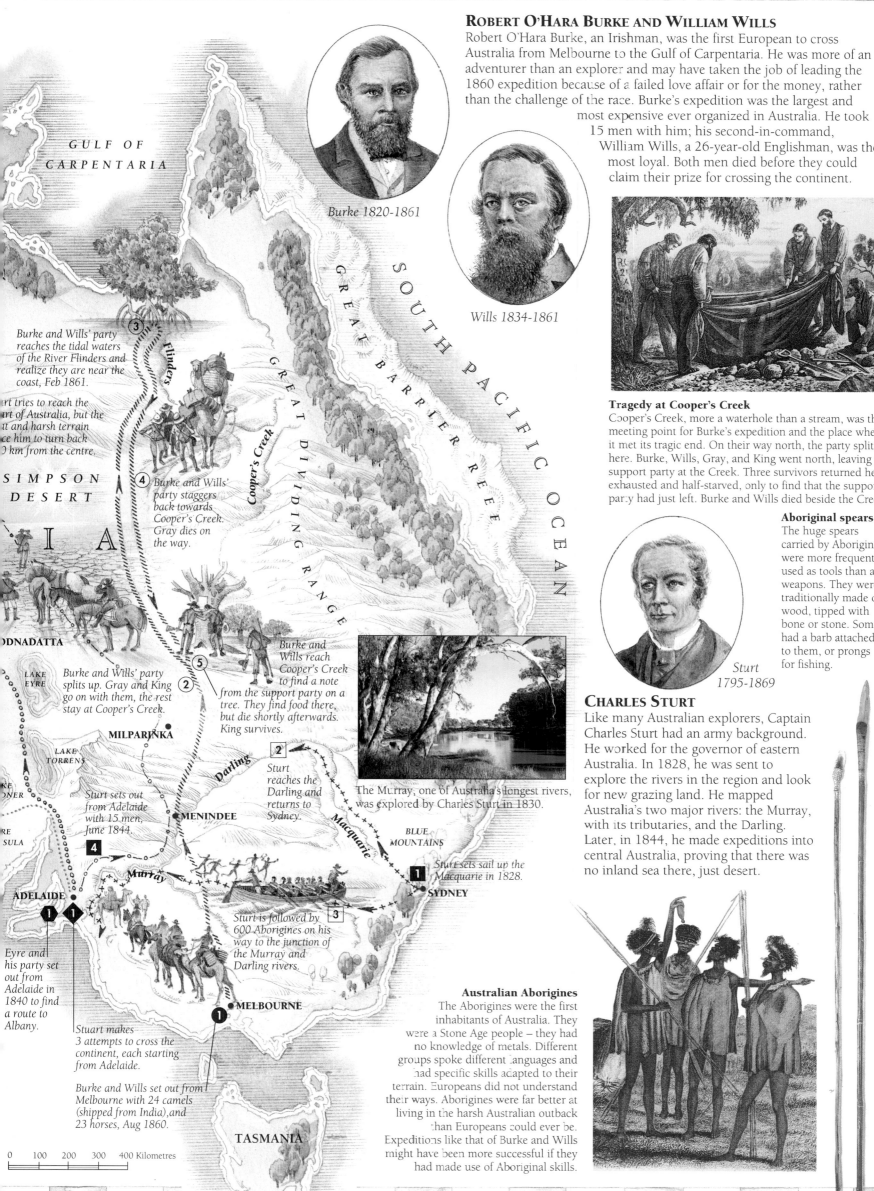

ROBERT O'HARA BURKE AND WILLIAM WILLS

Robert O'Hara Burke, an Irishman, was the first European to cross Australia from Melbourne to the Gulf of Carpentaria. He was more of an adventurer than an explorer and may have taken the job of leading the 1860 expedition because of a failed love affair or for the money, rather than the challenge of the race. Burke's expedition was the largest and most expensive ever organized in Australia. He took 15 men with him; his second-in-command, William Wills, a 26-year-old Englishman, was the most loyal. Both men died before they could claim their prize for crossing the continent.

Burke 1820-1861

Wills 1834-1861

Tragedy at Cooper's Creek
Cooper's Creek, more a waterhole than a stream, was the meeting point for Burke's expedition and the place where it met its tragic end. On their way north, the party split up here. Burke, Wills, Gray, and King went north, leaving a support party at the Creek. Three survivors returned here, exhausted and half-starved, only to find that the support party had just left. Burke and Wills died beside the Creek.

Aboriginal spears
The huge spears carried by Aborigines were more frequently used as tools than as weapons. They were traditionally made of wood, tipped with bone or stone. Some had a barb attached to them, or prongs for fishing.

Sturt 1795-1869

CHARLES STURT

Like many Australian explorers, Captain Charles Sturt had an army background. He worked for the governor of eastern Australia. In 1828, he was sent to explore the rivers in the region and look for new grazing land. He mapped Australia's two major rivers: the Murray, with its tributaries, and the Darling. Later, in 1844, he made expeditions into central Australia, proving that there was no inland sea there, just desert.

Map labels

GULF OF CARPENTARIA

SOUTH PACIFIC OCEAN

GREAT BARRIER REEF

GREAT DIVIDING RANGE

SIMPSON DESERT

Flinders

Cooper's Creek

③ Burke and Wills' party reaches the tidal waters of the River Flinders and realize they are near the coast, Feb 1861.

[...]rt tries to reach the [...]rt of Australia, but the [...]t and harsh terrain [...]e him to turn back [...] km from the centre.

④ Burke and Wills' party staggers back towards Cooper's Creek. Gray dies on the way.

ODNADATTA

LAKE EYRE

LAKE TORRENS

Burke and Wills' party splits up. Gray and King go on with them, the rest stay at Cooper's Creek.

② ⑤

MILPARINKA

Darling

Sturt sets out from Adelaide with 15 men, June 1844.

MENINDEE

④

Burke and Wills reach Cooper's Creek to find a note from the support party on a tree. They find food there, but die shortly afterwards. King survives.

② Sturt reaches the Darling and returns to Sydney.

Macquarie

BLUE MOUNTAINS

① Sturt sets sail up the Macquarie in 1828.

SYDNEY

Murray

ADELAIDE ① ①

Sturt is followed by 600 Aborigines on his way to the junction of the Murray and Darling rivers. ③

Eyre and his party set out from Adelaide in 1840 to find a route to Albany.

① MELBOURNE

Stuart makes 3 attempts to cross the continent, each starting from Adelaide.

Burke and Wills set out from Melbourne with 24 camels (shipped from India), and 23 horses, Aug 1860.

TASMANIA

0 100 200 300 400 Kilometres

The Murray, one of Australia's longest rivers, was explored by Charles Sturt in 1830.

Australian Aborigines
The Aborigines were the first inhabitants of Australia. They were a Stone Age people – they had no knowledge of metals. Different groups spoke different languages and had specific skills adapted to their terrain. Europeans did not understand their ways. Aborigines were far better at living in the harsh Australian outback than Europeans could ever be. Expeditions like that of Burke and Wills might have been more successful if they had made use of Aboriginal skills.

THE NATURALISTS

EUROPEANS HAD BEEN exploring the world at a rapid rate since the 15th century, but in the 18th century their style of exploration changed – it became more scientific. Earlier explorers had travelled in the hope of finding gold mines, valuable trade, fame, and land for their countries. Now explorers added the hope of new scientific discoveries to this list and their expeditions included scientists as well as sailors, soldiers, merchants, and adventurers. Their aim was to find out more about the wildlife of exotic tropical countries in southern Africa, Southeast Asia, and above all South America.

The first great scientific expedition to South America set out to record the shape and size of the Earth – the science known as geodesy. More importantly, though, it opened the eyes of naturalists (scientists interested in natural history – the study of wild animals and plants) to the unusual wildlife in the continent, especially in the huge tropical rainforests around the River Amazon.

Bonpland 1773-1858

Humboldt 1769-1859

ALEXANDER VON HUMBOLDT AND AIMÉ BONPLAND

Alexander von Humboldt, a German naturalist, was described by Charles Darwin as "the greatest scientific traveller who ever lived". He was interested in all aspects of natural history and was a fine writer. In 1797 he teamed up with a French naturalist, Aimé Bonpland, who specialized in botany (the study of plants). They made a scientific expedition to South America in 1799.

Bonpland's plants
In the days before photography, it was necessary for naturalists to be talented artists. This *Melastoma coccinea* is one of the fine drawings of plants painted by Bonpland in South America. He recorded over 3,000 new plant species and gathered many samples; the most important of these came from the cinchona tree. Its bark was used to develop quinine, a cure for the tropical disease malaria, which had killed many early explorers.

CHARLES-MARIE DE LA CONDAMINE
The French Academy of Sciences chose Charles-Marie de la Condamine to lead an expedition to South America in 1734. He was a brilliant mathematician with a special interest in geodesy. He had to settle an argument about the shape of the Earth by calculating the width of the Earth near the equator, while another expedition did the same in the Arctic. He became fascinated by South America's plant and animal life and stayed on for 10 years to study it.

La Condamine 1701-1774

Rubber
The strange elastic substance known as rubber comes from the rubber tree (left). Rubber is made from latex, a milky juice that is drained from the trunk of the tree and collected in pots. Columbus had seen South American people playing with a ball made from rubber, but La Condamine is said to have been the first explorer to take it back to Europe.

Humboldt and Bonpland set out to explore the Andes, April 1801.

La Condamine sets out from Cartagena in May 1735.

Humboldt and Bonpland sail along the River Magdalena, then ride up the mountains to Bogotá.

La Condamine first sees people collecting juice from rubber trees in the jungle near Manta.

The challenge of Chimborazo
In June 1802 Humboldt and Bonpland set off with a large party of men to climb Mount Chimborazo in the Andes. On the way they stopped to collect samples of the various plants growing in the fertile soil near the base of the volcanic mountain. At 5,800 m, very near to the top, they had to turn back due to lack of oxygen. They had achieved a world record, which was not broken for another 30 years.

Humboldt and Bonpland climb Mt Chimborazo.

La Condamine sails along the Amazon to the Atlantic Ocean.

Bonpland collects samples of the cinchona tree near Loja.

Spruce stays in Tarapoto for 2 years to study rubber trees.

La Condamine rides to Lima, then heads back to Cuenca.

Humboldt and Bonpland leave Lima and sail north, heading for Mexico.

PACIFIC OCEAN

CENTRAL AMERICA

ANDES MOUNTAINS

CARTAGENA
PORTOBELO
PANAMA
Magdalena
BOGOTÁ
QUITO
MT CHIMBORAZO
MANTA
GUAYAQUIL
CUENCA
Amazon
LOJA
Ucayali
TARAPOTO
TRUJILLO
Huallaga
LIMA

0 100 200 300 400 Kilometres

KEY TO MAP
CHARLES DE LA CONDAMINE	1735-44	**1** ○○○○○○
HUMBOLDT & BONPLAND	1799-1804	**1** ‖‖‖‖‖
WALLACE & BATES	1848-50	✦ -+++++
RICHARD SPRUCE	1849-64	**1** - - - -
ALFRED WALLACE	1850-52	▲ ⊕⊕⊕⊕
HENRY BATES	1850-59	◆ ○–○–○

HENRY WALTER BATES

Henry Bates, an Englishman, worked as a clerk, but had a keen interest in botany. He and Alfred Wallace were inspired to make their own expedition to South America by the writings of Humboldt and Darwin. Bates remained in the Amazon Basin for 11 years and only returned to England in 1859 for the sake of his health. He brought back 14,000 specimens, mostly insects, of which about half were unknown to European scientists.

Bates 1825-1892

Amazon toucans protest

Henry Bates came to know the rainforest better than any other European. He says in his book, *The Naturalist on the River Amazon*, that the forest is often very quiet and its animals hard to see. On one occasion, the peace and quiet were severely disrupted when he found himself surrounded by a flock of angry, screeching birds, protesting at his capture of one of them. They were curl-crested toucans, just one of many brilliantly-coloured birds of the forest that Bates saw near the River Negro. They would have been familiar to local people, but were completely unknown in Europe.

ALFRED RUSSEL WALLACE

Alfred Wallace, an English schoolmaster, was two years older than his friend Bates, with whom he shared a passion for natural history. On his expedition to South America, he took great trouble to collect live specimens on the River Uaupés, brought them all the way to the coast, but lost his entire collection when his ship caught fire.

Wallace 1823-1913

An expert's sketchbooks

Bates recorded all the insects he found. He painted them in perfect detail in his sketchbooks (left), then numbered and labelled each one.

RICHARD SPRUCE

Richard Spruce, an Englishman, was a teacher by profession, but his real love was botany. Before going to South America, he spent two years collecting plants in Spain, paying his expenses by selling his specimens. He sailed to South America on the same ship as Wallace's brother in 1849 and returned to England in 1864, with 30,000 plant specimens.

Spruce 1817-1893

CARACAS

CUMANÁ

1

Orinoco

Humboldt and Bonpland arrive at Cumaná, July 1799. They stop to collect plants.

ure

Humboldt and Bonpland encounter mosquitoes, and vampire bats on the River Orinoco. They reach the River Negro and turn back.

2

SAN ANTONIO

Negro

Orinoco

Wallace is startled by a jaguar, the great panther of South America.

2 UAUPÉS

upés

Wallace collects many plants and animals around the Uaupés and Negro rivers.

The River Amazon led naturalist explorers deep into the rainforest to search for exotic plants and animals.

Wallace and Bates travel up the Amazon to Manaus, where they part company, March 1850.

Negro

1

FONTE BOA

"EGA"

1

SÃO PAULO DE OLIVENÇA

Bates sails as far as São Paulo in a steamboat, 1857.

Bates stays near "Ega" for many years and collects thousands of insect specimens.

MANAUS

4

Spruce spends a year collecting plants and insects around Santarém.

2

SANTARÉM

Madeira

Tapajós

3 *Bates explores the River Tapajós from his base at Santarém.*

PARAMARIBO

5

La Condamine sails to Paramaribo and leaves for France, 1744.

ATLANTIC OCEAN

Wallace sails for England. His ship catches fire and all his specimens are destroyed. He is rescued after 9 days at sea.

3

Spruce arrives at Pará and sets off up the Amazon, heading for Santarém, Oct 1849.

BELÉM (Pará)

1 **1**

Wallace and Bates arrive at Pará, April 1848.

Amazon

Wallace and Bates spend 18 months collecting butterflies in the forests around Pará. They find 150 species in just 3 weeks.

2

Xingu

Tocantins

3 *Wallace and Bates go up the River Tocantins by canoe, then return to Pará.*

N
W E
S

SOUTH AMERICA

DARWIN AND THE BEAGLE

THE MAIN PURPOSE of the voyage of the *Beagle* was to survey and chart the seas around South America. However, it was the additional findings of Charles Darwin, the ship's naturalist, that brought fame to the expedition. During the voyage, Darwin gathered important evidence on which to base his theory of evolution. Evolution is the idea that all plants and animals have descended from earlier species and adapted over the years. Darwin did not invent this idea, but he was the first to explain how evolution works. His book on the subject, *On the Origin of Species,* shocked many people when it was published in 1859. Darwin was attacked for questioning the story of creation in the Bible – that all creatures were created in their present form by God.

Darwin 1809-1882

CHARLES DARWIN

Charles Darwin came from a large, wealthy English family. His father was a doctor and for a while he too studied medicine. He then trained to be a priest, but he abandoned that as well. His real interest was natural history (the study of plants and animals). In 1831, aged 23, he signed on as naturalist on the *Beagle.*

HMS Beagle

The *Beagle* was a small naval ship, which had been in use since 1825 and had already sailed around the world by the time Darwin joined the crew. For the 1831 voyage the *Beagle* was refitted at great cost, but with a crew of 74, space was cramped. Darwin lived and worked at one end of the chart room. He suffered from very bad seasickness and was always glad to reach a harbour.

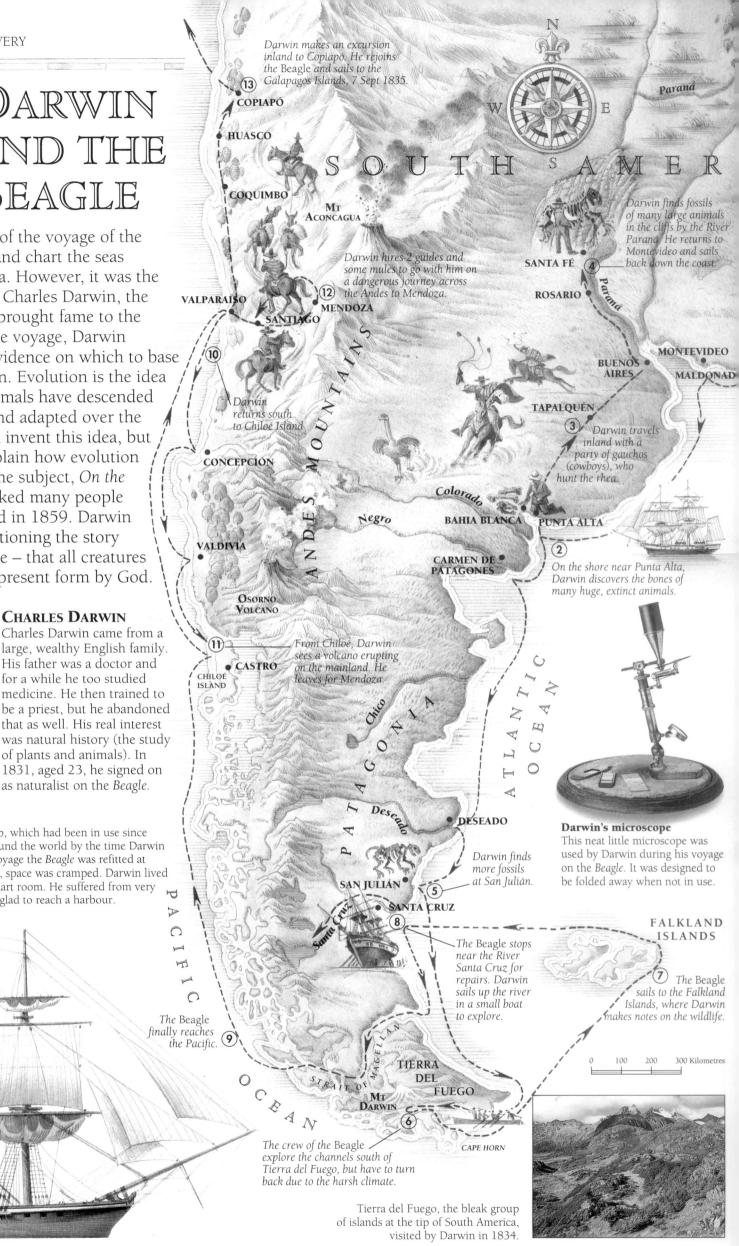

Darwin makes an excursion inland to Copiapó. He rejoins the Beagle and sails to the Galapagos Islands, 7 Sept 1835.

⑬ COPIAPÓ

HUASCO

COQUIMBO

MT ACONCAGUA

S O U T H   S   A M E R

Darwin hires 2 guides and some mules to go with him on a dangerous journey across the Andes to Mendoza.

VALPARAISO

⑫ MENDOZA

SANTIAGO

⑩

Darwin returns south to Chiloé Island

CONCEPCIÓN

VALDIVIA

OSORNO VOLCANO

⑪

CASTRO

CHILOÉ ISLAND

From Chiloé, Darwin sees a volcano erupting on the mainland. He leaves for Mendoza.

Darwin finds fossils of many large animals in the cliffs by the River Paraná. He returns to Montevideo and sails back down the coast.

SANTA FÉ ④

ROSARIO

Paraná

Parana

MONTEVIDEO

BUENOS AIRES

MALDONAD

TAPALQUÉN

③

Darwin travels inland with a party of gauchos (cowboys), who hunt the rhea.

Colorado

Negro

BAHIA BLANCA

CARMEN DE PATAGONES

PUNTA ALTA

②

On the shore near Punta Alta, Darwin discovers the bones of many huge, extinct animals.

A N D E S   M O U N T A I N S

P A T A G O N I A

Chico

Deseado

DESEADO

Darwin finds more fossils at San Julián.

SAN JULIÁN

⑤

SANTA CRUZ

⑧

Santa Cruz

A T L A N T I C   O C E A N

The Beagle stops near the River Santa Cruz for repairs. Darwin sails up the river in a small boat to explore.

FALKLAND ISLANDS

⑦

The Beagle sails to the Falkland Islands, where Darwin makes notes on the wildlife.

P A C I F I C   O C E A N

The Beagle finally reaches the Pacific.

⑨

STRAIT OF MAGELLAN

TIERRA DEL FUEGO

MT DARWIN

⑥

CAPE HORN

The crew of the Beagle explore the channels south of Tierra del Fuego, but have to turn back due to the harsh climate.

Darwin's microscope

This neat little microscope was used by Darwin during his voyage on the *Beagle.* It was designed to be folded away when not in use.

0   100   200   300 Kilometres

Tierra del Fuego, the bleak group of islands at the tip of South America, visited by Darwin in 1834.

A

❶ *The Beagle reaches South America and follows the coastline southwards.*

The voyage of the *Beagle* (1831-36)

The map on the right shows the complete voyage of the *Beagle*. In December 1831 the *Beagle* left the British Isles and sailed to South America, arriving in February 1832. Most of Darwin's work was done during the next three and a half years as the ship followed the coast of South America and headed west to the Galapagos Islands. The *Beagle* then crossed the Pacific to Tahiti and stopped briefly in New Zealand and Australia, before sailing to St Helena and back to South America. From there the course was set for home.

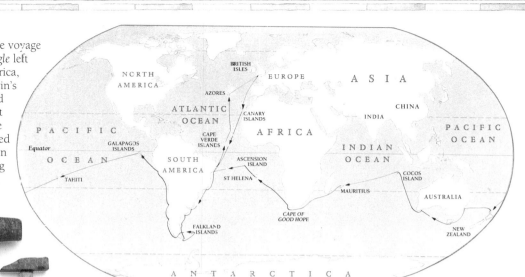

Darwin's tools

Darwin used these geologists' hammers to chip fossils from the rocks in South America.

Mylodon darwini

Darwin found the fossilized bones of this extinct giant sloth in the rocks above Punta Alta. This discovery was very important to him because it proved his theory that animals had gradually changed over the years to suit their environment. It also caused great excitement in England. Europeans had no idea that such huge prehistoric creatures had existed in South America. It is now known as the *Mylodon darwini*.

Explosions and tremors

While exploring the Andes Mountains, Darwin came very close to an erupting volcano. He also found seashells high in the mountains. This puzzled him until he realized that land is raised from the sea and then ground down again by the weather. Later, on the island of Chiloé, he felt the tremors of an earthquake. He describes this new experience in his diary: it "made me almost giddy". He noticed that after the earthquake, parts of the coast had been raised above sea level by two or three metres.

GALAPAGOS ISLANDS

These uninhabited islands, 1,000 km off the north west coast of South America, have a unique wildlife. They are named after the giant tortoises that are found there (Galapagos means "giant tortoise" in Spanish).

The Galapagos Islands (left), were formed by the eruption of volcanoes below sea-level. The landscape is dark with low cliffs and black boulders.

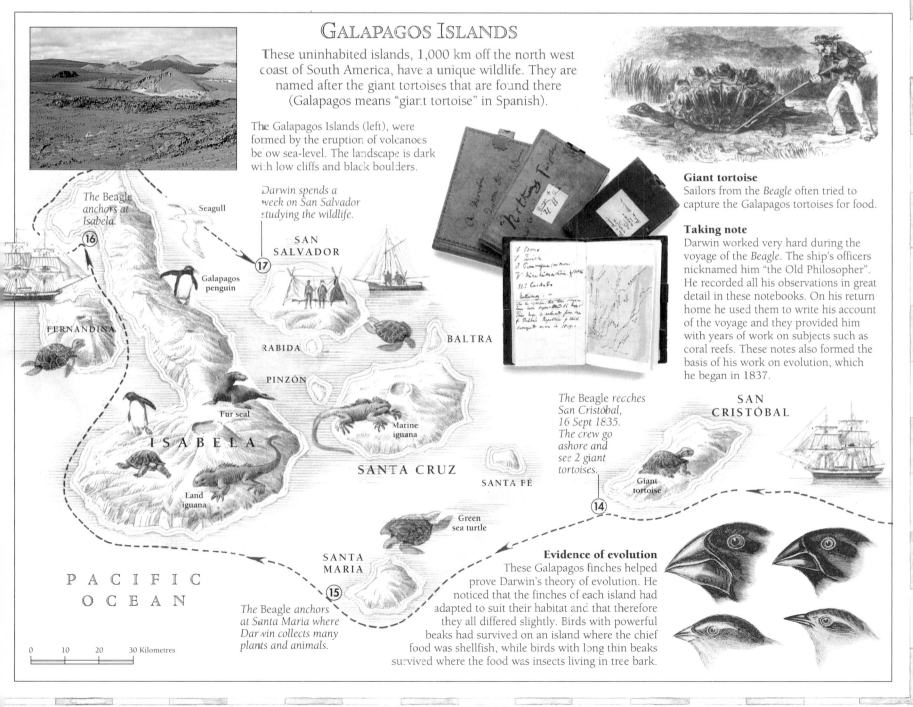

Giant tortoise

Sailors from the *Beagle* often tried to capture the Galapagos tortoises for food.

Taking note

Darwin worked very hard during the voyage of the *Beagle*. The ship's officers nicknamed him "the Old Philosopher". He recorded all his observations in great detail in these notebooks. On his return home he used them to write his account of the voyage and they provided him with years of work on subjects such as coral reefs. These notes also formed the basis of his work on evolution, which he began in 1837.

The Beagle anchors at Isabela.

⑯

Seagull

Darwin spends a week on San Salvador studying the wildlife.

SAN SALVADOR

⑰

Galapagos penguin

FERNANDINA

RABIDA

BALTRA

PINZÓN

Fur seal

Marine iguana

ISABELA

Land iguana

SANTA CRUZ

SANTA FÉ

The Beagle reaches San Cristóbal, 16 Sept 1835. The crew go ashore and see 2 giant tortoises.

SAN CRISTÓBAL

Giant tortoise

⑭

Green sea turtle

SANTA MARIA

⑮

The Beagle anchors at Santa Maria where Darwin collects many plants and animals.

PACIFIC OCEAN

0   10   20   30 Kilometres

Evidence of evolution

These Galapagos finches helped prove Darwin's theory of evolution. He noticed that the finches of each island had adapted to suit their habitat and that therefore they all differed slightly. Birds with powerful beaks had survived on an island where the chief food was shellfish, while birds with long thin beaks survived where the food was insects living in tree bark.

OCEAN EXPLORATION

OCEANOGRAPHY IS THE STUDY of the oceans and everything in them. It is quite a recent science, dating from about 1850. Before that, although sailors and fishermen knew a lot about the sea, few people had studied it. They did not have the equipment needed to study the ocean far below the surface. The ancient Greeks, who were interested in everything, wondered why the sea was salty and what caused the tides, but early travellers thought of the sea only as a way of getting to other lands – a useful but dangerous highway. No one sailed out of sight of land unless they had to. In the late 17th century the Scientific Revolution began to sweep Europe. People started to study nature in a scientific way and founded the modern sciences of physics, chemistry, and biology. The study and exploration of the oceans followed on from this. However, undersea exploration was still very difficult, except in shallow waters.

Monsters of the deep

The sea is a dangerous place, and early sailors imagined it was full of terrifying creatures. Mapmakers filled the blank spaces of the sea on their maps with gigantic sea serpents and whale-like creatures with huge teeth that could crush a ship. Many 16th-century sailors would tell of seeing mermaids combing their hair. Tales of mermaids and mermen came from all parts of the world. A "mermaid" was exhibited in London, England, as late as 1825, but she turned out to be a woman with a false tail.

Marsigli in the Mediterranean

Luigi-Ferdinando Marsigli, an Italian count, was the first serious undersea explorer. Working off the Mediterranean coast of France in 1706, he hired fishing boats and adapted the nets used by coral fishermen to collect samples of corals and other sea life. He then took these home to study under a microscope. He made fine drawings of his specimens, mapped the seabed, and measured the sea's temperature. His studies convinced him that corals and sponges were plants, but in fact they are animals.

Marsigli's drawing of coral

Marsigli's nets

The first page from Pelham Aldrich's journal of the voyage of the Challenger. Aldrich was a member of the crew.

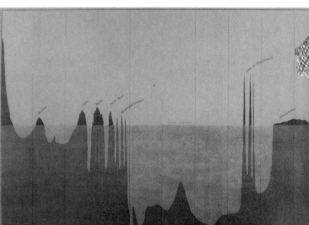

Maury in the Atlantic

Matthew Fontaine Maury was an American naval officer and an expert on navigation. In 1849 he launched the first major deep-sea survey. By the 1850s, study of the ocean floor was becoming important because of plans to lay a telegraph cable under the Atlantic. Maury's assistant, John Brooke, invented a "sounder", used to measure the depth of the ocean. By this means it was possible to draw a map of the ocean floor. Maury used this information to draw up a cross-section of the Atlantic (above), which he published in 1855.

Voyage of the *Challenger*

The first scientific conferences on oceanography were held in the late 19th century, and several expeditions were sent out to make studies of the oceans. One of these was the expedition on which Charles Darwin sailed in the *Beagle*. The voyage of the *Challenger* was a bigger project altogether. The *Challenger* was the first ship equipped for ocean exploration. It had two laboratories and the most advanced scientific equipment of the day, including this sounding machine (right) for measuring depth. Between 1872 and 1876 the *Challenger* sailed across the globe, through every ocean except the Arctic. The scientists on board investigated the water and its contents, as well as the reefs and islands. Their reports filled 50 volumes.

NORTH AMERICA — Halifax

BERMUDA · BEEBE 923 m 1934 · CANARY ISLANDS

HAWAIIAN ISLANDS · PUERTO RICO · ATLANTIC OCEAN · CAPE VERDE ISLANDS

BRITISH ISLES

PACIFIC OCEAN

Equator

TAHITI · SOUTH AMERICA

ROUTE OF THE CHALLENGER

Valparaiso · Montevideo

FALKLAND ISLANDS

ANTAR

Halley's diving bell

A diving bell was one of the earliest methods invented to enable divers to work underwater. It is like a cup turned upside down. As it is lowered through the water, the air inside is compressed, and more air has to be pumped in at the top to stop water filling the bell. The diving bell invented by Edmund Halley in 1690 was one of the first that worked well. It was made of wood, covered with lead to make it sink. The bell was supplied with air by a clever arrangement of barrels and leather pipes, and according to Halley, four men could stay on the seabed at a depth of 18 m for 90 minutes.

Diving helmet c.1840

Early diving equipment

In 1797 a German inventor, C. H. Kleingert, invented a very basic diver's suit. The upper half of the diver's body was enclosed in a sort of cylinder. Augustus Siebe invented a more open suit, like the one above, in about 1819. It allowed divers to move around more freely. The most important part was the heavy metal helmet. Air was pumped into the helmet from the surface, through a tube, and used air escaped below the neck. The air had to be pumped at the right pressure for the depth at which the diver was working. The pressure of the air escaping then prevented water from rising into the helmet.

Lead-soled diving boots c.1840

Beebe and the bathysphere

In 1934 the American inventor, Charles William Beebe, broke the record for deep-sea diving in a bathysphere, reaching a depth of 923 m off Bermuda in the Atlantic Ocean. The bathysphere (Greek for deep ball) was invented by Beebe (on the right) and his engineer Otis Barton. It was a large, hollow steel ball, less than 1.5 m in diameter, with windows of perspex. The bathysphere was lowered from a ship, using a powerful chain. Beebe and his successors discovered that some strange-looking creatures manage to live in the dark ocean depths.

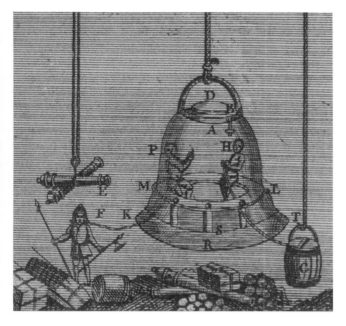

The aqualung

The aqualung was invented by the French oceanographer, Jacques Cousteau, in 1943. For the first time, divers could swim at depths of up to 30 m, without being attached by a line to a ship. The air supply is carried on the diver's back in cylinders, at high pressure. A tube takes the air to a mouthpiece, and a watertight mask with a glass front covers the eyes and nose. Thanks to the aqualung, any swimmer can explore the marvellous world below the surface of the water.

Compressed air cylinder

Face mask

The voyage of the *Trieste*

The bathyscaphe (deep boat), invented by Belgian scientist Auguste Piccard in 1953, was the first deep-water vessel, which could explore the deepest parts of the ocean. Piccard had the idea for designing it after studying airships. The U.S. navy bought Piccard's second bathyscaphe, the *Trieste II* (above), and in 1960 his son, Jacques, and naval officer Don Walsh descended more than 11,000 m to the bottom of the Marianas Trench. The trench lies in the Pacific and is the deepest known area in the oceans. From their steel ball beneath the craft they could see the extraordinary creatures that live at these depths.

THE MYSTERY OF AFRICA

TWO HUNDRED YEARS AGO Europeans knew nothing about Africa except for a few regions near the coast, even though large and powerful African empires had existed for more than a thousand years. Early European explorers did not like the look of Africa. Safe harbours were hard to find. The land was mostly desert or jungle and the rivers ended in huge, swampy deltas or were blocked by waterfalls. Apart from a little gold, ivory, and a few spices, the European ships that came to African ports after the 16th century wanted only slaves to sell for large profits in the American colonies. As late as the 18th century, most of Africa was still largely unknown to Europeans.

In 1788 the British botanist, Joseph Banks, who had crossed the Pacific with Captain Cook, founded the African Association to find out more about the interior of the continent. This marked the beginning of the serious exploration of Africa. The first expeditions were confined to the Sahara Desert and West Africa and the search for the source of Africa's longest river, the Nile.

A matter of guesswork
On this 16th-century French map of Africa, the coasts are quite accurate, thanks to the voyages of Portuguese explorers, but the interior was still a mystery, so the mapmaker filled the blank spaces with pictures. These imaginary details – a man with no head, one with six arms, and some very strange animals – show just how little Europeans knew about Africa. This map also illustrates the popular 16th-century belief that the Nile stretched the entire length of the country down to the "Mountains of the Moon".

MUNGO PARK

Park 1771-1806

The African Association hired Mungo Park, a Scotsman, to explore the River Niger in 1795. His ambition was to be famous, and when he returned to Britain having succeeded in reaching the Niger, he was disappointed that people did not recognize him as a great explorer. In 1805 he set out to follow the Niger to its source. The following year his canoe was ambushed by tribesmen and he was drowned.

René Caillié was the first European to cross the Sahara Desert in 1828.

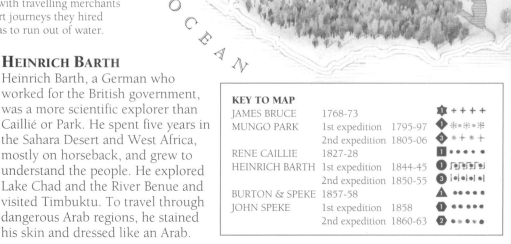

Park returns to Africa in May 1805 and sets out again to explore the River Niger.

Barth arrives in Rabat at the start of his first expedition, 1844.

Caillié crosses the Atlas Mountains in 6 weeks. He reaches Tangier and sails home for France.

Caillié leaves for Morocco with a caravan of 1,200 animals.

Caillié reaches Timbuktu and stays 2 weeks.

Park arrives at the River Gambia and sets out on horseback, Dec 1795.

Barth leaves Timbuktu and goes down the River Niger.

Park arrives at Segu and first sees the River Niger. He turns back due to floods.

Caillié arrives in West Africa, March 1827.

Park is attacked by tribesmen at Bussa Falls and drowns, 1806

The cruel desert
In the hot, dry Sahara Desert, Europeans were helpless on their own. On long journeys they teamed up with travelling merchants and their trade caravans (above); on short journeys they hired guides. The biggest danger they faced was to run out of water.

RENE CAILLIE

Caillié 1799-1838

In 1828 the Frenchman René Caillié became the first European to visit Timbuktu, in the Sahara Desert, and get back alive. In this region the people were Muslims and were hostile to Christians, so Caillié travelled in disguise, pretending to be an Arab. When he reached Timbuktu, he was disappointed to find that it was not a city of gold, as legend said, but of mud huts.

HEINRICH BARTH

Barth 1821-1865

Heinrich Barth, a German who worked for the British government, was a more scientific explorer than Caillié or Park. He spent five years in the Sahara Desert and West Africa, mostly on horseback, and grew to understand the people. He explored Lake Chad and the River Benue and visited Timbuktu. To travel through dangerous Arab regions, he stained his skin and dressed like an Arab.

KEY TO MAP			
JAMES BRUCE	1768-73		
MUNGO PARK	1st expedition	1795-97	
	2nd expedition	1805-06	
RENE CAILLIE	1827-28		
HEINRICH BARTH	1st expedition	1844-45	
	2nd expedition	1850-55	
BURTON & SPEKE	1857-58		
JOHN SPEKE	1st expedition	1858	
	2nd expedition	1860-63	

RICHARD BURTON

Richard Burton was a great scholar and a fearless explorer. He was already an experienced traveller when he began to explore East Africa. In 1853 Burton had dressed as an Arab and visited the holy city of Mecca, near Jedda, which is forbidden to non-Muslims. For his explorations in East Africa, he chose John Hanning Speke as a companion.

Burton 1821-1890

The hunt for the source of the Nile
Burton and Speke set out together to search for the source of the Nile in 1857. They travelled west as far as Lake Tanganyika where Burton fell seriously ill. Speke continued the search alone. He headed north and found a large lake, which he named Victoria. He left, certain that this was the true source of the Nile. Burton refused to believe him. In 1860 Speke set out for the lake again with James Grant. This time a local African tribe (left) blocked his path and delayed him for five months. Finally, in 1862, he found the source of the Nile at Ripon Falls to the north of the lake.

JOHN HANNING SPEKE

Burton's companion, John Hanning Speke, was a quiet-spoken young Englishman who liked the outdoor life. He had cherished for a long time an ambition to travel through Africa. In 1855 Speke finished a 10-year tour of duty with the Indian Army and was free to start making plans to travel in Africa. Within two years, he was exploring East Africa with Burton.

Speke 1827-1864

Speke's sketches
Drawings of gazelles from Speke's sketchbook. One species, Grant's gazelle, is named after the companion Speke took with him on his expedition of 1860.

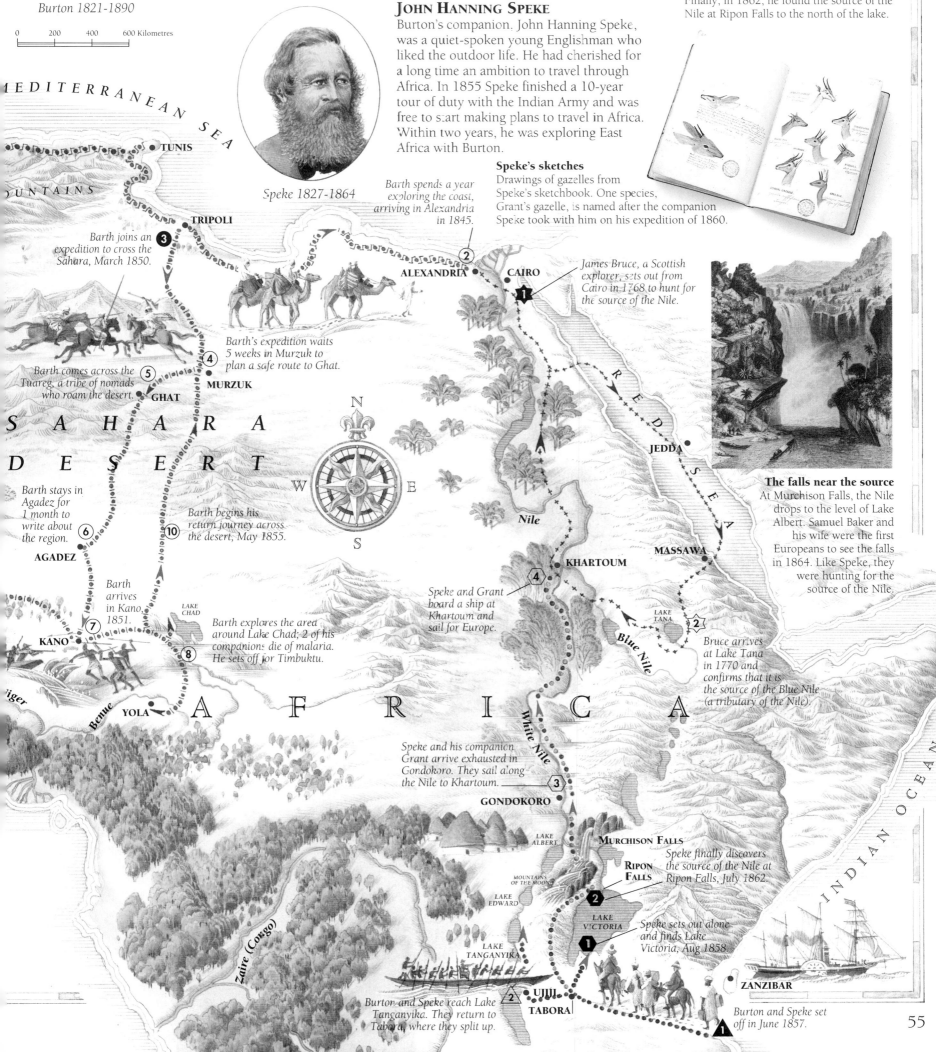

Scale: 0 200 400 600 Kilometres

Richard Burton

Barth spends a year exploring the coast, arriving in Alexandria in 1845.

James Bruce, a Scottish explorer, sets out from Cairo in 1768 to hunt for the source of the Nile.

Barth joins an expedition to cross the Sahara, March 1850. **3**

TUNIS
TRIPOLI
ALEXANDRIA
CAIRO **1**

Barth's expedition waits 5 weeks in Murzuk to plan a safe route to Ghat. **4**

Barth comes across the Tuareg, a tribe of nomads who roam the desert. **5**
GHAT
MURZUK

SAHARA DESERT

Barth stays in Agadez for 1 month to write about the region. **6**
AGADEZ

Barth begins his return journey across the desert, May 1855. **10**

Barth arrives in Kano, 1851. **7**
KANO

LAKE CHAD

Barth explores the area around Lake Chad; 2 of his companions die of malaria. He sets off for Timbuktu. **8**

YOLA

A F R I C A

Nile

KHARTOUM

Speke and Grant board a ship at Khartoum and sail for Europe. **4**

JEDDA

MASSAWA

LAKE TANA
2

Blue Nile

The falls near the source
At Murchison Falls, the Nile drops to the level of Lake Albert. Samuel Baker and his wife were the first Europeans to see the falls in 1864. Like Speke, they were hunting for the source of the Nile.

Bruce arrives at Lake Tana in 1770 and confirms that it is the source of the Blue Nile (a tributary of the Nile).

White Nile

Speke and his companion Grant arrive exhausted in Gondokoro. They sail along the Nile to Khartoum. **3**
GONDOKORO

LAKE ALBERT

MURCHISON FALLS
RIPON FALLS

Speke finally discovers the source of the Nile at Ripon Falls, July 1862.

MOUNTAINS OF THE MOON

LAKE EDWARD

2

LAKE VICTORIA

1

Speke sets out alone and finds Lake Victoria, Aug 1858

LAKE TANGANYIKA

Burton and Speke reach Lake Tanganyika. They return to Tabora, where they split up. **2**
UJIJI
TABORA

Zaire (Congo)

ZANZIBAR

Burton and Speke set off in June 1857. **1**

INDIAN OCEAN

MEDITERRANEAN SEA

RED SEA

55

LIVINGSTONE AND STANLEY

THE EXPLORER John Hanning Speke described Africa as an upside-down soup plate. There is a rim of flat land near the coast and then the ground rises sharply; the interior is mostly level. European explorers of the continent did not have to climb many mountains, but they faced plenty of difficulties, notably disease, hunger, starvation, drought, robbery, and rebellion. They endured these hardships in their determination to explore the great African rivers – the pathways to the interior. Of all the Europeans to explore Africa's rivers during the 19th century, David Livingstone and Henry Morton Stanley are the best known. Livingstone, a Scottish missionary, followed the course of the Zambezi and also searched for the source of the Nile. Stanley, a journalist, followed the last great river to be explored by a European, the Zaire (then called the Congo), from its tributaries in the middle of the continent for about 3,220 km to the sea.

ATLANTIC OCEAN

DAVID LIVINGSTONE

At the age of 10, David Livingstone was working in a cotton mill near Glasgow. At 28 he arrived in southern Africa as a missionary, a qualified doctor and minister. He hoped to improve the life of the Africans with the benefits of European knowledge and trade. From 1853 to 1856 he crossed the continent, following the River Zambezi to the sea. From 1858 to 1864 he explored the Shire, Lake Nyasa, and the Ruvuma. He died while searching for the source of the Nile.

Livingstone 1813-1873

The curse of slavery

At the time Livingstone was in Africa, African natives were still being captured by Arabs for slavery (left), even though the slave trade had been banned in Europe. Livingstone hated slavery, but he realized to his horror that his expeditions were helping the traffic of human beings by opening up new routes to the interior. For 30 years he fought hard to end the Arab slave trade. Africa's main slave market in Zanzibar was closed a month after his death in 1873.

Exploring the Zambezi

Livingstone gave such a good report of the Zambezi that the British government sent an official expedition there, putting Livingstone in command and giving him the title of consul. This time his wife, Mary, went with him. The expedition was not a great success. Fierce rapids on the Zambezi prevented it from being the "highway" into Africa that Livingstone had hoped.

Finding the way

Livingstone took this compass with him on his expedition to the River Zambezi. The government paid for all his equipment, including a steamboat.

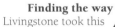

A famous meeting

In 1871 an American newspaper hired Stanley to look for Livingstone, who had disappeared. Rumours had reached Zanzibar of an old, sick white man seen near Lake Tanganyika. Stanley set off with 200 porters – the largest expedition anyone had seen in Africa. After a long trek he entered Ujiji with guns blazing and the United States' flag waving. When Livingstone appeared, Stanley was overwhelmed. He took off his hat and asked politely, "Dr Livingstone, I presume?"

Stanley 1841-1904

HENRY MORTON STANLEY

Henry Morton Stanley, an American, was an adventurer. Unlike David Livingstone, his main interests were not geography or African people, but fame and fortune. His expedition across Africa and down the River Congo was large and well armed but was often attacked. Livingstone had travelled almost alone. As Stanley had said grimly, "my methods will not be Livingstone's."

Different styles

These are the hats worn by David Livingstone (left) and Henry Morton Stanley (right) at their famous meeting at Ujiji on 10 November 1871.

Livingstone's last expedition

Livingstone refused to go back to England with Stanley and, though sick, set off towards the River Luapula, which he thought would lead to the Nile (in fact, it led to the Congo). It was the rainy season, and he had to be carried through the swamps around Lake Bangweulu. Early one morning in May 1873, his men found him kneeling as if in prayer. He was dead. Following his last wishes, his heart was buried in Africa and his body was carried back to Zanzibar and shipped home.

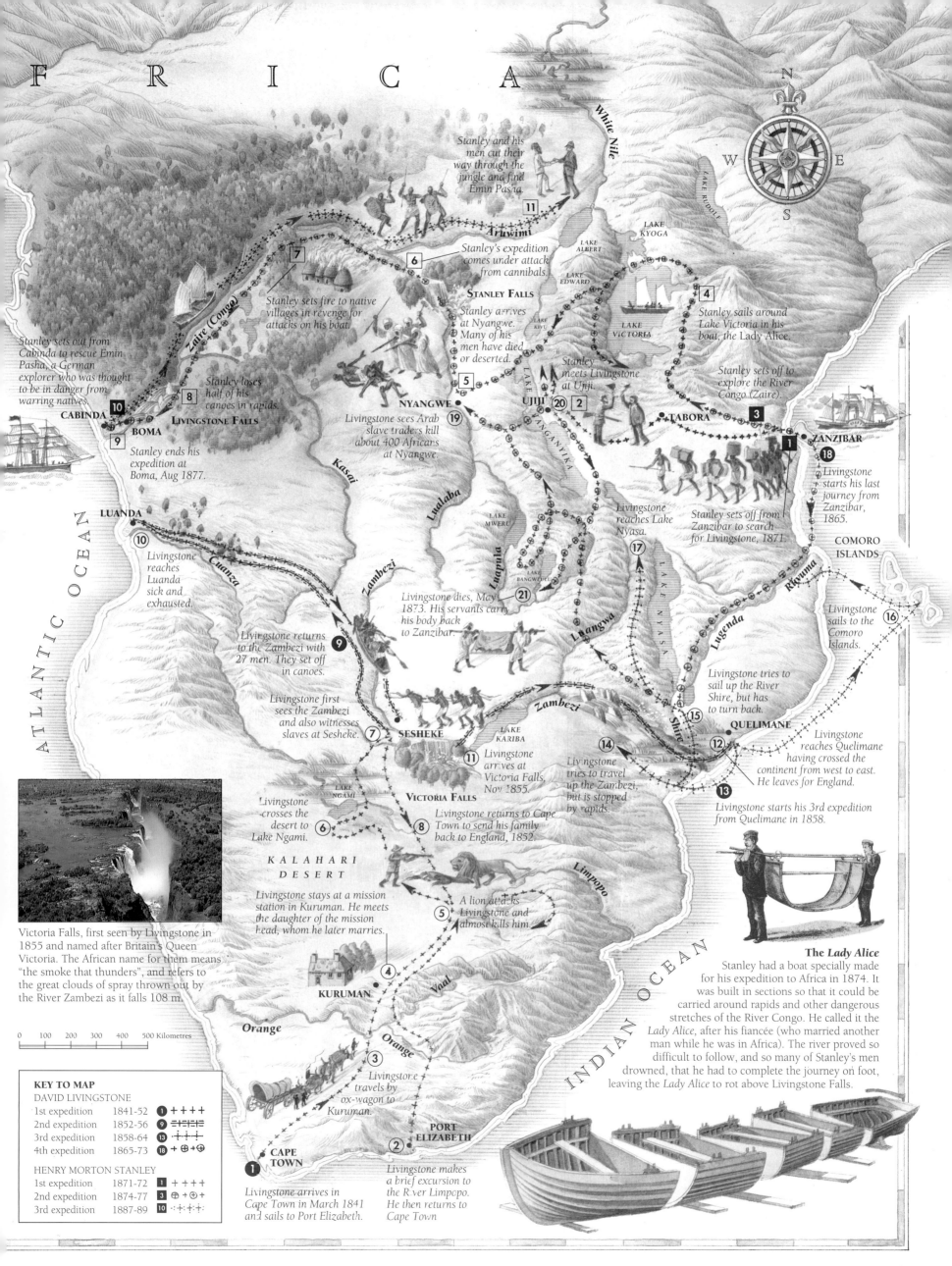

F R I C A

Stanley and his men cut their way through the jungle and find Emin Pasha.

11

Stanley's expedition comes under attack from cannibals.

Stanley sets fire to native villages in revenge for attacks on his boat.

7

6

STANLEY FALLS

Stanley arrives at Nyangwe. Many of his men have died or deserted.

5

Stanley sets out from Cabinda to rescue Emin Pasha, a German explorer who was thought to be in danger from warring natives.

10

8

Stanley loses half of his canoes in rapids.

LIVINGSTONE FALLS

CABINDA

BOMA

9

Stanley ends his expedition at Boma, Aug 1877.

LUANDA

10

Livingstone reaches Luanda sick and exhausted.

NYANGWE

19

Livingstone sees Arab slave traders kill about 400 Africans at Nyangwe.

Livingstone reaches the Zambezi with 27 men. They set off in canoes.

9

Livingstone dies, May 1873. His servants carry his body back to Zanzibar.

21

Livingstone first sees the Zambezi and also witnesses slaves at Sesheke.

7

SESHEKE

Livingstone crosses the desert to Lake Ngami.

6

Livingstone arrives at Victoria Falls, Nov 1855.

11

VICTORIA FALLS

Livingstone returns to Cape Town to send his family back to England, 1852.

8

Victoria Falls, first seen by Livingstone in 1855 and named after Britain's Queen Victoria. The African name for them means "the smoke that thunders", and refers to the great clouds of spray thrown out by the River Zambezi as it falls 108 m.

Livingstone tries to travel up the Zambezi, but is stopped by rapids.

14

Livingstone tries to sail up the River Shire, but has to turn back.

15

QUELIMANE

12

Livingstone reaches Quelimane having crossed the continent from west to east. He leaves for England.

13

Livingstone starts his 3rd expedition from Quelimane in 1858.

Livingstone sails to the Comoro Islands.

16

LAKE VICTORIA

4

Stanley sails around Lake Victoria in his boat, the Lady Alice.

Stanley sets off to explore the River Congo (Zaire).

3

TABORA

Stanley meets Livingstone at Ujiji.

20 **2**

UJIJI

Livingstone reaches Lake Nyasa.

17

Stanley sets off from Zanzibar to search for Livingstone, 1871.

1

ZANZIBAR

18

Livingstone starts his last journey from Zanzibar, 1865.

COMORO ISLANDS

Livingstone stays at a mission station in Kuruman. He meets the daughter of the mission head, whom he later marries.

4

A lion attacks Livingstone and almost kills him.

5

KALAHARI DESERT

KURUMAN

3

Livingstone travels by ox-wagon to Kuruman.

2

Livingstone makes a brief excursion to the River Limpopo. He then returns to Cape Town.

CAPE TOWN

1

Livingstone arrives in Cape Town in March 1841 and sails to Port Elizabeth.

PORT ELIZABETH

The Lady Alice
Stanley had a boat specially made for his expedition to Africa in 1874. It was built in sections so that it could be carried around rapids and other dangerous stretches of the River Congo. He called it the Lady Alice, after his fiancée (who married another man while he was in Africa). The river proved so difficult to follow, and so many of Stanley's men drowned, that he had to complete the journey on foot, leaving the Lady Alice to rot above Livingstone Falls.

ATLANTIC OCEAN

INDIAN OCEAN

0 100 200 300 400 500 Kilometres

KEY TO MAP
DAVID LIVINGSTONE
1st expedition	1841-52	**1**	++++
2nd expedition	1852-56	**9**	≒≒≒
3rd expedition	1858-64	**13**	+++
4th expedition	1865-73	**18**	+ ⊕ + ⊕

HENRY MORTON STANLEY
1st expedition	1871-72	**1**	+ + + +
2nd expedition	1874-77	**3**	⊕ + ⊕ +
3rd expedition	1887-89	**10**	÷+÷+

TO THE NORTH POLE

BY THE BEGINNING OF the 19th century, European explorers had learned a great deal about the Arctic region without penetrating its centre. They had mapped most of the coasts and islands, and they knew that ice covered a large part of the Arctic Ocean. By the end of the century, the Arctic had become the focus of an international race as explorers set out for the North Pole, which lies at its centre.

Travel in the Arctic was both difficult and dangerous. The ice is not smooth and flat like that on a pond: the pressure of ice floes banging against each other as they are carried along by ocean currents raises high, jagged ridges about 10 m high. Elsewhere, ice floes may suddenly break apart, blocking the way forward by a "lead" – a channel of open water. Explorers often made slow progress because the ice was drifting in the opposite direction from the way they were going. Weather conditions were also hazardous due to sudden blizzards or thick fog. These dangers brought suffering, defeat, and death to many of the explorers who set out to conquer the North Pole.

Ideas about the North Pole
In earlier times, people had some strange ideas about the North Pole. This map was drawn by Nicholas of Lynn, a monk who lived in England during the 14th century. He thought that the Pole was a magnetic rock in the middle of a whirlpool and that it was surrounded by land, neatly divided into quarters by rivers. Even in the 19th century, many people still believed that there was land, rather than just ice, at the North Pole.

CHARLES FRANCIS HALL
In 1860 a middle-aged American publisher who had never seen an iceberg in his life set off for the Arctic. Hall's first expedition consisted of just one man – himself. He made three expeditions altogether. On the third, in 1871, he managed to get farther north than anyone before him, but he died on board his ship, *Polaris*, a few weeks later.

Hall 1821-1871

Hall and the Inuit
The Inuit (Eskimos) are the native inhabitants of the Arctic regions. Traditionally, they lived by hunting animals, such as caribou, seals, and whales, often killing them with harpoons made from antler. The Inuit used the skins of these animals to make clothing, tents, and boats called kayaks. They travelled on sledges drawn by dogs. Hall was one of the first explorers to make friends with the Inuit and copy their ways of dealing with the intense cold of the Arctic. He also studied their language. Here, he learns how to drive a sledge drawn by dogs. But not all Inuit customs were easy to follow. It took all his courage to try their favourite soup of hot seal's blood.

Food for survival
Pemmican is made of dried, pounded meat mixed with melted fat. It was invented by the Indians of northern Canada. Explorers often ate pemmican on Arctic expeditions because it is rich in calories, which help to keep the body warm. It also lasts for years. This tin comes from an expedition more than 100 years ago.

Kit for the cold
Early explorers were ill prepared for the extreme cold of the Arctic – they wore the same kind of clothes there that they wore at home. In the 19th century they realized that the fur clothes worn by the Inuit, such as this sealskin hood and mitten, were much warmer. The Inuit seldom suffered from frostbite.

ROBERT PEARY
American Arctic explorer Robert Peary was a naval officer, an engineer, and a keen naturalist. He was also very ambitious and was determined to be the first man to reach the North Pole. In 1891, he made his first journey to the Arctic, accompanied by his young wife and by his servant and friend Matthew Henson, the first black Arctic explorer. Peary made eight expeditions to the Arctic in total.

Peary 1856-1920

To the Pole by balloon
In 1897 Salomon Andrée, a Swedish engineer, tried to reach the North Pole in his balloon, *Øernen* (Eagle). He took off from the island of Spitsbergen, travelled for about two days, then disappeared. What happened remained a mystery until 1930, when the bodies of Andrée and his companions were discovered. A camera was also found. This photograph of the grounded balloon was on Andrée's film.

Peary at the Pole
In 1909 Peary returned from his eighth Arctic expedition, claiming that he had reached the North Pole. He took this photograph of Henson and their four Inuit companions at the spot he said was the Pole. Some people refused to believe that Peary had actually reached the North Pole, especially as he managed to travel back to his base in just over two weeks. His claim was generally accepted, but the argument about whether or not Peary did get to the Pole still goes on today. Some modern Arctic explorers say he could not have travelled so fast.

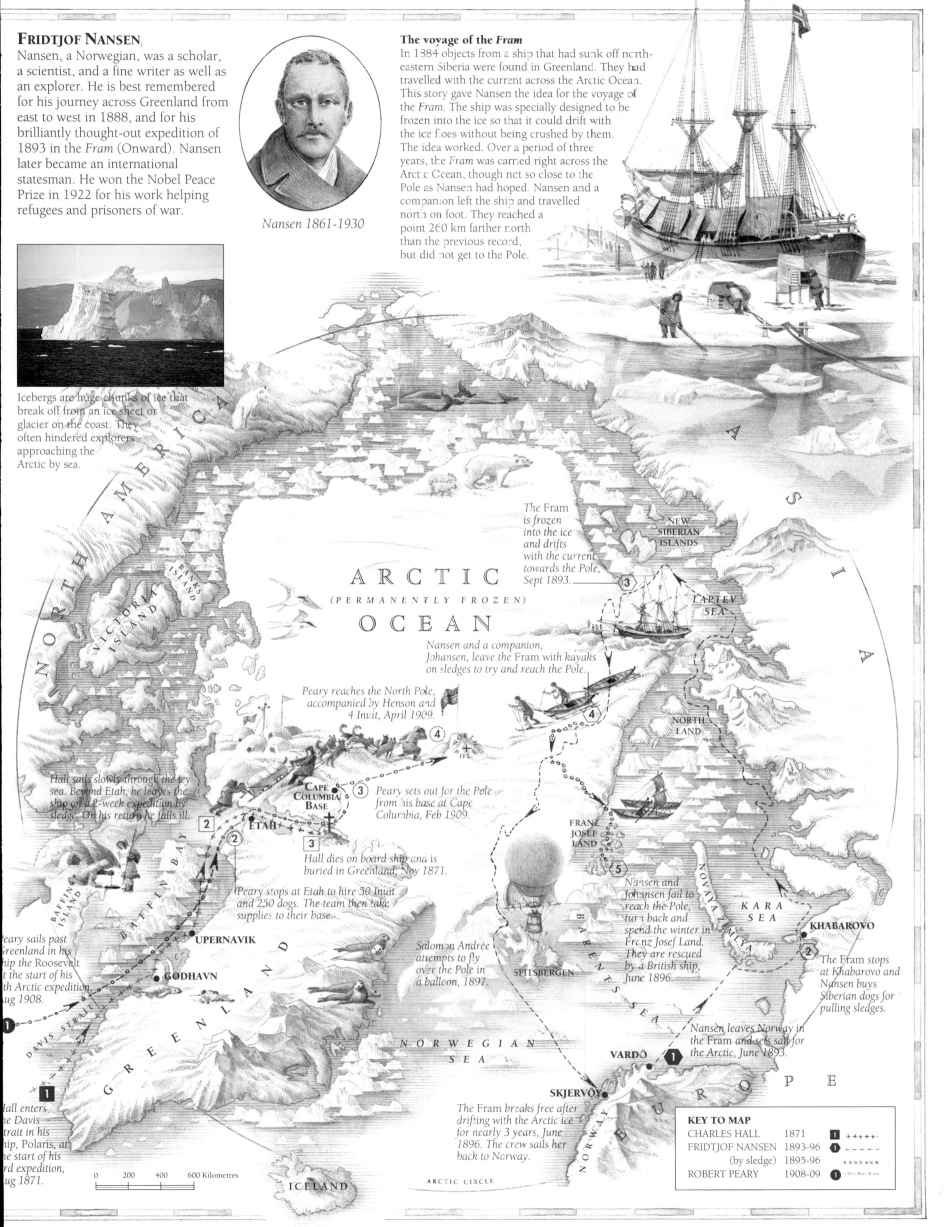

FRIDTJOF NANSEN

Nansen, a Norwegian, was a scholar, a scientist, and a fine writer as well as an explorer. He is best remembered for his journey across Greenland from east to west in 1888, and for his brilliantly thought-out expedition of 1893 in the *Fram* (Onward). Nansen later became an international statesman. He won the Nobel Peace Prize in 1922 for his work helping refugees and prisoners of war.

Nansen 1861-1930

Icebergs are huge chunks of ice that break off from an ice sheet or glacier on the coast. They often hindered explorers approaching the Arctic by sea.

The voyage of the *Fram*

In 1884 objects from a ship that had sunk off north-eastern Siberia were found in Greenland. They had travelled with the current across the Arctic Ocean. This story gave Nansen the idea for the voyage of the *Fram*. The ship was specially designed to be frozen into the ice so that it could drift with the ice floes without being crushed by them. The idea worked. Over a period of three years, the *Fram* was carried right across the Arctic Ocean, though not so close to the Pole as Nansen had hoped. Nansen and a companion left the ship and travelled north on foot. They reached a point 260 km farther north than the previous record, but did not get to the Pole.

NORTH AMERICA

BANKS ISLAND

VICTORIA ISLAND

ARCTIC

(PERMANENTLY FROZEN)

OCEAN

The Fram is frozen into the ice and drifts with the current towards the Pole, Sept 1893.

NEW SIBERIAN ISLANDS

A S I A

LAPTEV SEA

Nansen and a companion, Johansen, leave the Fram with kayaks on sledges to try and reach the Pole.

Peary reaches the North Pole, accompanied by Henson and 4 Inuit, April 1909.

NORTH LAND

NORTH POLE

Hall sails slowly through the icy sea. Beyond Etah, he leaves the ship on a 2-week expedition by sledge. On his return he falls ill.

CAPE COLUMBIA BASE

Peary sets out for the Pole from his base at Cape Columbia, Feb 1909.

ETAH

FRANZ JOSEF LAND

Hall dies on board ship and is buried in Greenland, Nov 1871.

Peary stops at Etah to hire 50 Inuit and 250 dogs. The team then take supplies to their base.

Salomon Andrée attempts to fly over the Pole in a balloon, 1897.

SPITSBERGEN

Nansen and Johansen fail to reach the Pole, turn back and spend the winter in Franz Josef Land. They are rescued by a British ship, June 1896.

KARA SEA

NOVAYA ZEMLYA

BARENTS SEA

KHABAROVO

The Fram stops at Khabarovo and Nansen buys Siberian dogs for pulling sledges.

BAFFIN ISLAND

BAFFIN BAY

Peary sails past Greenland in his ship the Roosevelt at the start of his 5th Arctic expedition, Aug 1908.

UPERNAVIK

GODHAVN

DAVIS STRAIT

Hall enters the Davis Strait in his ship, Polaris, at the start of his 3rd expedition, Aug 1871.

GREENLAND

NORWEGIAN SEA

Nansen leaves Norway in the Fram and sets sail for the Arctic, June 1893.

VARDØ

SKJERVØY

The Fram breaks free after drifting with the Arctic ice for nearly 3 years, June 1896. The crew sails her back to Norway.

NORWAY

EUROPE

0   200   400   600 Kilometres

ICELAND

ARCTIC CIRCLE

KEY TO MAP		
CHARLES HALL	1871	++++++
FRIDTJOF NANSEN	1893-96	
(by sledge)	1895-96	
ROBERT PEARY	1908-09	

TO THE SOUTH POLE

THE SOUTH POLE, unlike the North Pole, is covered by land. It lies in the centre of the vast frozen continent of Antarctica – the coldest place in the world. Antarctica was also the last continent in the world to be explored.

Captain James Cook was the first to cross the Antarctic Circle in 1773, though he did not see land. It wasn't until 1820 that British and American seal-hunters first spotted the Antarctic Peninsula. In the 1840s three expeditions – led by Jules Dumont d'Urville for France, Charles Wilkes for the United States, and James Ross for Britain – began to chart the coasts of Antarctica. They had difficulty finding the edge of the land because it is overlapped in so many places by a great ice sheet.

Serious scientific exploration of the Antarctic got under way in the 1890s. Then, at the start of this century, explorers from many nations made heroic attempts to triumph over the hardships of the severe climate, hoping to reach the end of the Earth – the South Pole.

Ideas about the South Pole

The ancient Greeks believed that there must be a vast "southern continent" around the South Pole. Their ideas influenced European mapmaking for centuries. At various times, Europeans drew New Guinea, Australia and New Zealand as part of it. This French map of 1739, though inaccurate, comes closer to the truth. Antarctica, the real southern continent, is shown correctly as an ice-covered landmass, but the mapmaker has invented a sea dividing it in two.

JAMES CLARK ROSS

Ross, a British naval officer, spent many years exploring the Arctic before leading an expedition to the Antarctic in 1839. He was the first explorer to find a way through the floating pack-ice (thick sea-ice) in his ships *Erebus* and *Terror*. Many of the areas he discovered in the region are now named after him – Ross Island, Ross Sea, and the Ross Ice Shelf.

Ross 1800-1862

Famous chronometer

This chronometer, belonging to the Royal Observatory at Greenwich, London, was taken on two British Antarctic expeditions. The Observatory lent it to Ernest Shackleton in 1907, and to Robert Scott for his *Terra Nova* expedition in 1910.

Scott 1869-1912

Amundsen 1872-1928

ROALD AMUNDSEN

As a young man, Amundsen, a Norwegian, gave up his studies in medicine to join an expedition to the Antarctic and then devoted the rest of his life to the challenges of polar exploration. By the time he set out for the South Pole in 1911, he had already established two records: in 1898 he was among the first to spend a winter in Antarctica and in 1906 he became the first person to sail through the North-West Passage.

ROBERT FALCON SCOTT

Scott was a young naval officer, chosen to lead the British *Discovery* expedition to Antarctica in 1901. In the next three years, he gained great experience of polar survival and travelled farther south across Antarctica than any explorer before him. By the *Terra Nova* expedition in 1910, he had come to think of the Antarctic as "his" continent and had set his heart on being the first person to reach the South Pole.

Scott's disappointment

Scott left his base by the Ross Sea 10 days after Amundsen, taking 10 men, 10 ponies and 23 dogs. The ponies soon died in the harsh climate. The weather conditions were terrible and there were huge obstacles to overcome, such as the Beardmore Glacier. By the time they had climbed it, the expedition was reduced to 2 sledges and 5 men, supplies were low and they were suffering from frostbite. They finally reached the Pole on 17 January 1912, only to find that Amundsen had beaten them. In this photograph of the team, taken by remote control, the bitter disappointment is plain on their tired faces. Scott and his men all died on the return journey.

Sledgemeter

Scott's *Terra Nova* expedition of 1911 took a very scientific approach to exploring the Antarctic. This device, which works like the milometer on a bicycle, was attached to the back of one of his sledges to measure the distance travelled. His base by the Ross Sea is about 1,470 km from the South Pole.

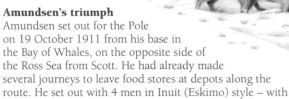

Amundsen's triumph

Amundsen set out for the Pole on 19 October 1911 from his base in the Bay of Whales, on the opposite side of the Ross Sea from Scott. He had already made several journeys to leave food stores at depots along the route. He set out with 4 men in Inuit (Eskimo) style – with sledges pulled by dogs. They made fast progress, even when climbing the Axel Heiberg Glacier and arrived triumphantly at the South Pole on 14 December.

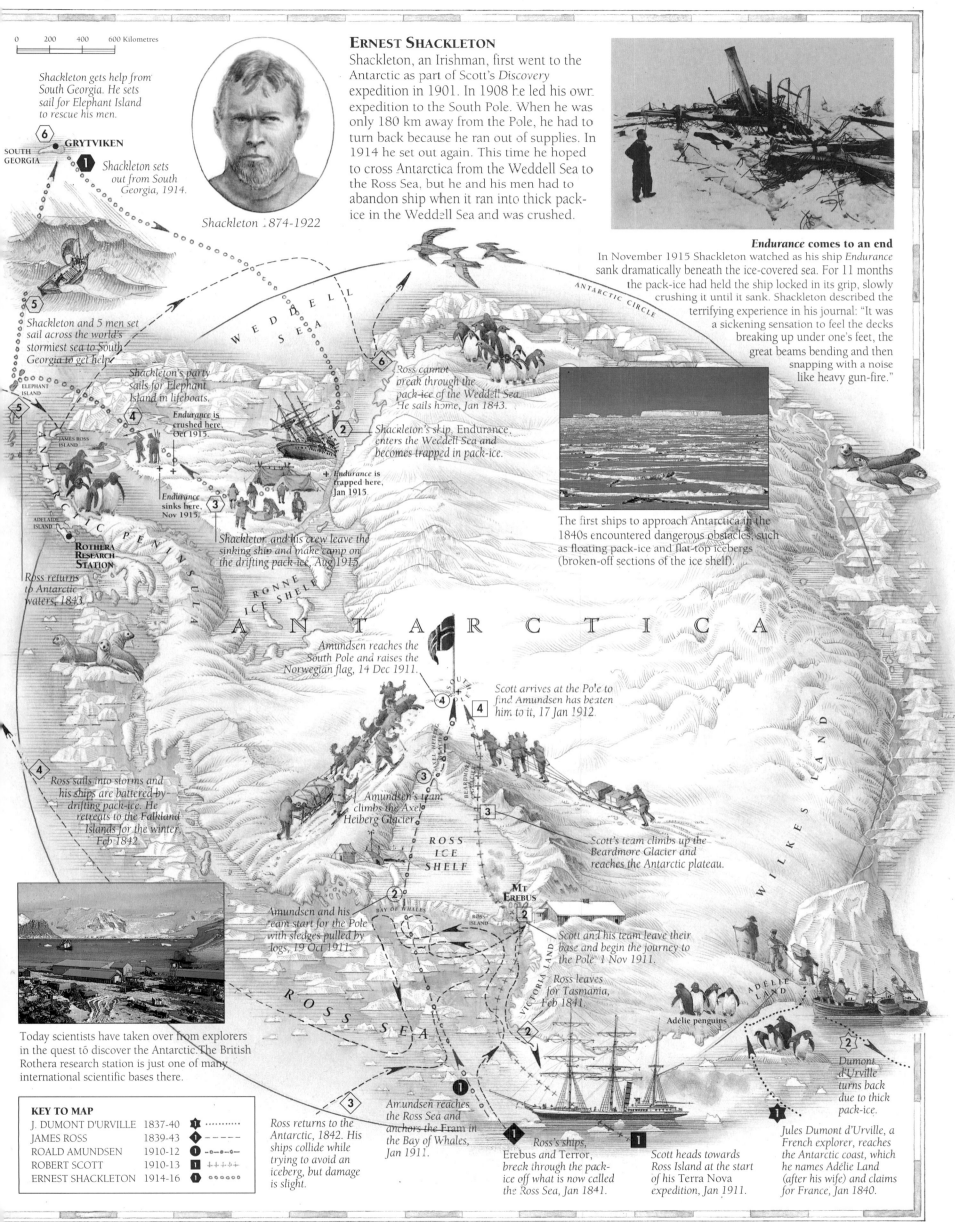

0 200 400 600 Kilometres

Shackleton gets help from South Georgia. He sets sail for Elephant Island to rescue his men.

6 GRYTVIKEN

SOUTH GEORGIA **1** *Shackleton sets out from South Georgia, 1914.*

5

Shackleton and 5 men set sail across the world's stormiest sea to South Georgia to get help.

ELEPHANT ISLAND

5

Shackleton's party sails for Elephant Island in lifeboats.

4

JAMES ROSS ISLAND

Endurance is crushed here, Oct 1915.

Endurance sinks here, Nov 1915.

Endurance is trapped here, Jan 1915.

3

Shackleton and his crew leave the sinking ship and make camp on the drifting pack-ice, Aug 1915.

ADELAIDE ISLAND

ROTHERA RESEARCH STATION

A N T A R C T I C   P E N I N S U L A

Ross returns to Antarctic waters, 1843.

4

Ross sails into storms and his ships are battered by drifting pack-ice. He retreats to the Falkland Islands for the winter, Feb 1842.

Today scientists have taken over from explorers in the quest to discover the Antarctic. The British Rothera research station is just one of many international scientific bases there.

ERNEST SHACKLETON

Shackleton, an Irishman, first went to the Antarctic as part of Scott's *Discovery* expedition in 1901. In 1908 he led his own expedition to the South Pole. When he was only 180 km away from the Pole, he had to turn back because he ran out of supplies. In 1914 he set out again. This time he hoped to cross Antarctica from the Weddell Sea to the Ross Sea, but he and his men had to abandon ship when it ran into thick pack-ice in the Weddell Sea and was crushed.

Shackleton 1874-1922

W E D D E L L   S E A

ANTARCTIC CIRCLE

6 *Ross cannot break through the pack-ice of the Weddell Sea. He sails home, Jan 1843.*

2 *Shackleton's ship, Endurance, enters the Weddell Sea and becomes trapped in pack-ice.*

***Endurance* comes to an end**

In November 1915 Shackleton watched as his ship *Endurance* sank dramatically beneath the ice-covered sea. For 11 months the pack-ice had held the ship locked in its grip, slowly crushing it until it sank. Shackleton described the terrifying experience in his journal: "It was a sickening sensation to feel the decks breaking up under one's feet, the great beams bending and then snapping with a noise like heavy gun-fire."

The first ships to approach Antarctica in the 1840s encountered dangerous obstacles, such as floating pack-ice and flat-top icebergs (broken-off sections of the ice shelf).

RONNE ICE SHELF

A N T A R C T I C A

Amundsen reaches the South Pole and raises the Norwegian flag, 14 Dec 1911.

4

SOUTH POLE

4 *Scott arrives at the Pole to find Amundsen has beaten him to it, 17 Jan 1912.*

3

AXEL HEIBERG GLACIER

Amundsen's team climbs the Axel Heiberg Glacier

BEARDMORE GLACIER

3

Scott's team climbs up the Beardmore Glacier and reaches the Antarctic plateau.

ROSS ICE SHELF

W I L K E S   L A N D

MT EREBUS

2

ROSS ISLAND

BAY OF WHALES

2

Amundsen and his team start for the Pole with sledges pulled by dogs, 19 Oct 1911.

Scott and his team leave their base and begin the journey to the Pole, 1 Nov 1911.

VICTORIA LAND

Ross leaves for Tasmania, Feb 1841.

R O S S   S E A

2

ADÉLIE LAND

Adélie penguins

2 *Dumont d'Urville turns back due to thick pack-ice.*

3

Amundsen reaches the Ross Sea and anchors the Fram in the Bay of Whales, Jan 1911.

Ross returns to the Antarctic, 1842. His ships collide while trying to avoid an iceberg, but damage is slight.

1 *Ross's ships, Erebus and Terror, break through the pack-ice off what is now called the Ross Sea, Jan 1841.*

1 *Scott heads towards Ross Island at the start of his Terra Nova expedition, Jan 1911.*

1 *Jules Dumont d'Urville, a French explorer, reaches the Antarctic coast, which he names Adélie Land (after his wife) and claims for France, Jan 1840.*

KEY TO MAP

J. DUMONT D'URVILLE	1837-40	**1** ·········
JAMES ROSS	1839-43	**1** – – – –
ROALD AMUNDSEN	1910-12	**1** -o-o-o-
ROBERT SCOTT	1910-13	**1** ++++
ERNEST SHACKLETON	1914-16	**1** ooooo

61

MODERN EXPLORATION

THANKS TO THE DETERMINATION of generations of explorers, there is almost no place on Earth that is still unknown and unnamed. We know what lies in the oceans' depths, and at the top of the highest mountain. Maps chart the dry rocks of the world's deserts and the glaciers of the coldest polar regions. Even the Earth's gravity has not stopped explorers from heading out into space. As distant places have become more familiar, the nature of exploration has changed. The challenge is no longer to discover the world's wild places. Today, explorers are trying to understand the Earth and its climate, and the living things that inhabit its surface. For millions of years, the Earth's natural systems have lived in delicately balanced harmony. Exploration itself does little to upset this balance. But when people move into newly discovered areas they cause permanent changes. The explorers of the past showed our ancestors the wonders of the Earth. The duty of explorers today is to discover how to preserve these wonders for future generations.

Mountain exploration
Mountaineering is not just a sporting challenge. Much of the world's population lives in or depends on mountainous areas. Research in the Himalayas (above) has shown that the destruction of forests on mountain slopes can erode the soil, and cause flooding. Scientists hope to learn more about the Earth's geology and origins by studying and measuring the tiny shifts of the bare rocks on mountaintops.

The world's highest peak
Mount Everest in the Himalayas, on the border of Nepal and Tibet, is the world's highest mountain. On 29 May 1953, New Zealander Sir Edmund Hillary (born 1919) and Nepalese mountaineer Tenzing Norgay (1914-1986) became the first explorers to reach the 8,848 m summit. They carried oxygen cylinders to help them breathe in the thin air at the top of the mountain. The picture above shows Hillary and Tenzing near the summit of Mount Everest.

Race for the rainforest
The tropical rainforests provide a good example of the difference between exploration and understanding. Explorers have visited some of the most remote rainforests, yet scientists still know little about the "canopy", the blanket of foliage that towers 30 m above the forest floor. One way to get a closer look is to build walkways (left). Scientists estimate that most of the plant or animal species living in the canopy have not yet been identified or given a name. Unfortunately, time is running out for those who want to study the forests and the creatures that live in them. Commercial development is destroying 110,000-150,000 sq km of rainforest per year.

KEY TO MAP
- Rainforests
- Deserts
- Mountains

NORTH AMERICA

ATLANTIC OCEAN

PACIFIC OCEAN

Tropic of Cancer

Equator

Tropic of Capricorn

AMAZON BASIN

SOUTH AMERICA

ANDES MOUNTAINS

ANTARCTIC

The Maracá Project
On a remote, uninhabited Brazilian island close to the border with Venezuela, scientists from the Royal Geographical Society (above) measure new saplings in the rainforest. This is part of an adventurous project to study the forest and the plants and animals that inhabit it. Maracá is an island in the River Uraricoera, which feeds the giant River Amazon. The RGS established a base there to study the regrowth of the forest, its soil and water, land development, and insect life. A research station was built at the eastern end of the island and the project, which began in 1987, went on for more than a year.

People of the rainforest
For native people (below) whose home is the rainforest, its destruction means the end of cultures and traditions that have lasted since prehistoric times. These tribal people have learned to use their forest environment in a way that does not harm it; but they do not yet know how to use political systems to stop farmers, miners, timber companies, and engineers destroying the forest for short-term profit.

The conquest of space

Until the 1950s, exploration was limited to the Earth. But in 1957 the Soviet Union launched the first space satellite, *Sputnik I*. It was only the size of a football, and all it could do was send out radio signals. But within four years both the United States and the Soviet Union had launched spacecraft with crews. The race to be first into space started with the Moon (right). Initially it was a military contest, not a scientific one, but today space exploration is for more peaceful scientific reasons.

Destination Moon

In 1959, the Soviet Union sent a spacecraft to the Moon; nine years later two American astronauts were the first human beings to leave Earth's orbit and fly to the Moon. Though they circled it they did not land. That honour went to Neil Armstrong and Edwin ("Buzz") Aldrin (both born in 1930) when they walked on the Moon's surface on 20 July 1969. Now that the Moon has been visited, space scientists today are concentrating on building space stations closer to Earth, and sending space probes to find out more about regions of space much farther away.

An eye in the sky

Earth resource satellites such as the United States Landsat series (left) orbit 700 to 900 km high with their sensors directed towards the Earth. The signals they send back are intercepted at ground stations where computers turn them into photographs. These highly accurate photographs help scientists to map the world's most remote regions, to look for mineral resources, and to track the spread of pollution and crop disease. The pictures (like the one below of a mountainous area of China) do not show the true colours of the Earth's surface, but use contrasting colours so that various features show up clearly.

Deserts and dry areas

Exploration of desert areas began long ago, but scientific research is a more recent development. One in eight of the world's people lives in a desert area, or an area of low rainfall. As this population increases, it puts greater pressure on the scarce natural resources in these areas. As a result of overgrazing and too many trees being cut down, over a million square kilometres of farm land turns to desert every five years. Scientists have set up desert research stations to look at how to reverse this process.

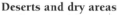

Wahiba Sands project

In 1985 the Wahiba Sands Project in eastern Oman made a detailed study of every aspect of this vast desert region. The government of Oman and the Royal Geographical Society assembled a team of more than 40 specialists, which included biologists, economists and sociologists. Together they established a "field university" in the desert.

Polar research

Because of an international treaty, the Antarctic region is devoted to peaceful scientific purposes. Today 24 countries have scientific bases in Antarctica. Despite the emptiness of this frozen wilderness, the southern polar region has tremendous scientific importance. For example the ice itself is like an environmental data-bank. Its layers form a record of the composition of the snow that has fallen on the continent over the last 160,000 years. By studying cores drilled from the 4.5 km-thick ice sheet, scientists can find out how the climate and atmosphere have changed throughout this period.

Antarctic pioneers

The last place on Earth to be explored was the cold, hostile "ice desert" of the Antarctic. The first expedition to cross the continent took place as recently as 1958. Dr Vivian Fuchs (born 1908) led the 12-member British Commonwealth Trans-Antarctic Expedition. The group began the crossing from the Shackleton Base on the Weddell Sea close to the coast of Argentina and the Falkland Islands. Light aircraft dropped supplies onto the ice, and checked the route ahead, and the expedition travelled in tracked Sno-Cat vehicles (left) with one dog-sled. They reached the South Pole on 19 January 1958, and completed the crossing to Scott Base 3,475 km away, a little more than three months after setting off. In 1990 an international team repeated this amazing feat using dog-sleds.

Youth exploration

The North Pole does not have a treaty for environmental protection, as the South Pole does. Scientists are concerned that commercial development could damage the Arctic forever. To draw attention to this, 22 young people from 15 nations took part in the Icewalk Student Expedition in 1989. They journeyed to the North Pole to study the Arctic through lectures and scientific studies on the ice.

INDEX

ACKNOWLEDGMENTS

Dorling Kindersley would like to thank the following:
Richard Platt for writing pages 14-15, 42-3 and 62-3.
Emma Johnson, Susan Peach and Constance Novis for
editorial assistance. Hussain Mohamed, Lester Cheeseman
and Marcus James for design assistance. Anna Kunst, Zoe
Wilkinson and Eric Smith for research.

Consultant Richard Humble

Map consultant Andrew Heritage

Picture research Kathy Lockley

Inset maps and globes Aziz Khan

Index Hilary Bird

Picture credits
Abbreviations / key: r=righ:, l=left, t=top, c=centre, b=below.

Andreemuseet, Granna: 58bl
Arctic Camera: 26c
Aspect Picture Library: 34cr, 34cl
B.A.S./C. Gilbert: 61bl
Biofotos/Heather Angel: 57bl
Bodleian Library, Oxford: 12bl
Bridgeman Art Library:16tr/City of Bristol Museum & Art
    Gallery: 26t, 45c
British Library: 5cr, 9br, 14br, 15tr, 16br, 22c, 30tc, 30tl, 34b,
    36tr, 52tl & r, 58ttr, 60tr
E.T. Archive: 12tr
Mary Evans Picture Library: 7tr, 17bl, 17tc, 30bc, 52tc
Werner Forman Archive: 10cr
Photographie Giraudon/Musee Guimet: 41br
Susan Griggs Agency/Leon Schadeberg:17cr
Sonia Halliday: 2br, 12tc
Robert Harding Picture Library: 10br, 12cl, 14bl, 14cl, 17tl,

18tl, 35br, 52bc, 54c, 54tr, 61cr, 62tl, 62bl
Michael Holford: 7br, 15c
Hulton Picture Company: 11tl, 14tr, 51cr, 53tl
Hutchison Picture Library: 19bl
Kon-Tiki Museet 19tr
Mansell Collection: 15ct, 20br, 39br
N.A.S.A: 63tl, 63tc
National Maritime Museum: 4cl, 20c, 20cl, 20bl, 20br, 21bl,
    21cl, 21c, 21cr, 21tr, 21tc, 21tl, 22bc, 25cr, 27cr, 27tc, 28c,
    31br, 31tr, 42tr, 45bl, 45bc, 45br, 45tr, 53cr, 53tr, 58c, 58cr/
    The Honourable Lady Rowley: 45cr
Natural History Museum: 45cl, 48cr, 48bl, 49cr
N.H.P.A./A.N.T. Otto Rogge: 44br/ Ted Hutchison: 46tr/ Jocelyn
    Burt: 47c, 50br
N.H.P.A./Haroldo Palo: 51cl
Operation Raleigh Picture Library: 62bl
Photo Researchers Inc/Paolo Koch: 8c
Planet Earth Pictures/Andrew Mounter: 25bl/ M. A. Ogilvie:
    29cl/Flip Schulke: 53bl/ Rod Salm 59tl
Popperfoto: 30bl, 53br

Project Icewalk: 63bl
Rijksmuseum, Amsterdam: 43c
Ann Ronan Picture Library: 19tl
Royal Geographical Society: 3br, 60bc, 61tr, 62cb, 62ct, 63br,
    63rcb, 63rc
Science Museum Library: 7cr
Science Photo Library: 21br
South American Pictures: 35cl
Still Pictures/Mark Edwards: 49c
Stofnun Arna Magnussonar (Iceland Manuscript Institute): 10t
Syndication International: 23br, 26bl, 35bl, 36c/ J. Judkin
    Memorial Fund, Freshford Manor, Bath: 36bc/Nasjonal galleriat,
    Oslo: 11tc/ Natural History Museum: 48tc/Royal Geographical
    Society: 58bc
TASS: 29br
Tokyo National Museum: 9cr
TRH Pictures/N.A.S.A: 63tr
Weidenfeld & Nicholson/Denver Public Library: 39br
Wildlight Photo Agency/ David Moore: 42c
ZEFA: 13cl, 23bl